D1431830

HAUNTED
PLANTATIONS
—— OF THE ——
SOUTH

ABOUT THE AUTHOR

Richard Southall is the author of *How to be a Ghost Hunter* (2003) and *Haunted Route 66* (2013). He has also written articles for a number of periodicals, including *FATE Magazine*. To reflect his interest in writing about the unknown, Richard is a current member of the Horror Writers' Association.

In addition, he has been a featured guest on several national and international radio shows including the *X-Zone Radio Show* with Rob McConnel, *Shadows of the Paranormal*, *Edge of the Unknown*, and *Spirited History with Leanne and Angela*.

Richard lives in northern West Virginia with his family, where he has worked for over ten years as a substance abuse therapist. He is actively involved in his community and is a current member of the Freemasons and Scottish Rite.

RICHARD SOUTHALL

HAUNTED
PLANTATIONS
—— OF THE ——
SOUTH

Llewellyn Publications
Woodbury, Minnesota

FIRST EDITION
First Printing, 2015

Cover art by Shutterstock/179003066/©Netfalls-Remy Musser
Cover design by Kevin R. Brown
Editing by Patti Frazee
Interior photos courtesy of the Library of Congress

Llewellyn is a registered trademark of Llewellyn Worldwide Ltd.

Library of Congress Cataloging-in-Publication Data
Southall, Richard.
  Haunted plantations of the South / Richard Southall. — First edition.
     pages   cm
  Includes bibliographical references.
  ISBN 978-0-7387-4024-9
  1. Haunted plantations--Southern States. 2. Ghosts—Southern States.
  I. Title.
  BF1477.2.S68 2015
  133.1'22—dc23
                              2015003843

Llewellyn Publications
A Division of Llewellyn Worldwide Ltd.
2143 Wooddale Drive
Woodbury, MN 55125-2989
www.llewellyn.com

Printed in the United States of America

Other Books by Richard Southall

How to be a Ghost Hunter

Haunted Route 66: Ghosts of America's Legendary Highway

CONTENTS

INTRODUCTION

I have always been intrigued by and attracted to the antebellum South, the Civil War, the Reconstruction Era, and the lifestyles that were representative of each of those very different times. In recent years, I became even more interested in those time periods after tracing my genealogy to distant family members directly involved in the Civil War and the Reconstruction.

Unlike my previous book, *Haunted Route 66: Ghosts of America's Legendary Highway,* this project was a bit more challenging. With *Haunted Route 66,* many of the ghost stories I wrote about were found on a 2,448-mile highway that has been in existence since 1926. While conducting research for *Haunted Plantations of the South,* I soon realized that I was dealing with plantation histories, ghost stories, and legends that in some cases went back three hundred years or more. Also, there were nearly a thousand plantations throughout the eastern and southern states. With such a large number of plantations to choose from, it was difficult to determine which of these plantations to include while writing *Haunted Plantations of the South.*

I decided to limit the number of ghost stories in this book to give the reader a better idea of individual plantations. Rather than simply writing down descriptions of hauntings, I wanted to focus on the brief history of each plantation. I think this may offer a better understanding of why a place became haunted.

As I conducted research for *Haunted Plantations of the South*, I came across statistics for casualties of a particular battle, or the number of slaves that a certain planter had on his property. I thought that the statistics, although necessary to show the scale of a particular event, depersonalize the individual. These statistics include men who were somebody's husband, son, father, and sibling. As such, each person has a story to tell, and to simply offer a statistic of an event prevents their stories from being heard. If a casualty list has ten thousand names on it, then there are ten thousand stories that can be told. This is one of the main reasons I wrote *Haunted Plantations of the South*—I wanted to give a voice to some of these people.

The stories of the slaves, planters, and soldiers often converge on the plantation. Slaves often spent several years working on the plantations with very little recognition for their hard work. Planters spent a great deal of time and money making certain that their plantations were successful. During the Civil War, Union and Confederate soldiers often took over the mansions and used them as field hospitals to tend to and sometimes bury their wounded comrades. For all people involved, the plantation was a very emotionally charged location.

Many of the legends and ghost stories in *Haunted Plantations of the South* may vary somewhat from versions you have heard, especially if you live near a particular plantation. This is to be expected. As people share a particular story about a location, additional details are added or removed, which can lead to the emergence of several different versions of the same story.

Chapter 1 describes the different types of plantation architectural styles and reasons why a plantation may be haunted. Each of the subsequent chapters contains several entries that offer a brief history, ghost stories, and legends associated with plantations that have a reputation for being haunted.

I certainly hope that you enjoy *Haunted Plantations of the South*. Whether you are reading this book from a historical perspective or as a paranormal enthusiast, I would like to dedicate this book to you, the reader. By reading the stories in the pages that follow, you are helping keep the memories alive of the people I have written about. I would like to also dedicate *Haunted Plantations of the South* to the memories of the planters, soldiers, and slaves who have made this book possible.

— ONE —

HISTORY OF PLANTATIONS

"I want the old days back again and they'll
never come back, and I am haunted by the memory of them
and of the world falling about my ears."

—MARGARET MITCHELL, *Gone with the Wind*

Haunted Plantations of the South is a book about the lifestyle that Margaret Mitchell so eloquently described in this quote from *Gone with the Wind*. Mitchell's book gives the reader a realistic glimpse of how chaotic life was for everybody during and after the Civil War.

Unlike *Gone with the Wind*, *Haunted Plantations of the South* focuses on a brief history of nearly one hundred separate plantations from seven different states. In order to truly appreciate the ghost stories and legends associated with the plantations, it is important to delve into the history of each location.

It is also important to understand that there were several different types of plantations that existed in the South. Just as most plantations had a distinct name, each plantation had its own individual history. Of course, these histories are accompanied by many legends and ghost stories that make each plantation unique.

In the late 1600s, the first plantations established in America were founded by settlers who were given land grants by the British crown for their dedication, courage, and loyalty. Often these land grants consisted of thousands or even tens of thousands of acres. These men often cleared the land and established plantations. By the way, the oldest plantation on American soil is Shirley Plantation, established in 1638 in colonial Virginia.

Most of the early plantations in America were dedicated to growing tobacco, which was fairly easy to raise and very profitable for the plantation owners, known as planters. In time, other plantations were founded and they focused on crops such as rice, cotton, indigo, and sugar cane.

The Houmas/Burnside Plantation, located in Darrow, Louisiana, is an example of the French Colonial style of architectural design. Courtesy Library of Congress.

Cultivation and harvesting of crops grown on these enormous plantations took considerable resources and manpower. The resources originally were imported from overseas, but soon stores and other businesses were built near some of the most successful plantations. The manpower was found in the form of slaves purchased by the planters. Some of the larger towns and cities in the southern states are named after a plantation, a planter, or an individual who first established a business in the area.

Many planters were so successful in managing their plantations that they became some of the wealthiest and most influential men in all of early America. As a result of this power, many planters entered the political arena on a local, state, or national level. Several of the founding fathers, such as George Washington and Thomas Jefferson, were some of the most successful plantation owners ever.

Although plantations represented affluence and wealth among the different planters, there was also a great deal of strife and conflict that could not be ignored. Diseases such as tuberculosis, typhoid fever, and yellow fever were contracted by both slaves and plantation owners. Because of the widespread prevalence of these diseases and limited knowledge of hygienic medical practices, it was not uncommon for plantation owners to die before they reached forty years of age.

It was common for wealthier plantation owners to have both a main plantation house and a more remote summer house located a great distance from the plantation proper. One of the original reasons for a retreat was so that the plantation owners and their families and friends could remove themselves from exposure to diseases that sometimes ran rampant in the areas where many of the plantations were located.

To truly appreciate the role of plantations in American history, it is important to know exactly what a plantation was. Most historians agree that in order to be considered a plantation, the property had to consist of a minimum of 600 acres and have at least twenty slaves to work the property. According to the National Register of Historic Places, there were between 650 and 1,000 plantations that met that criteria, and they were scattered throughout eighteen states. The plantations covered in this book will include those found in Alabama, Georgia, Louisiana, Mississippi, North Carolina, South Carolina, and Virginia.

PLANTATION PERIODS

There are two major time periods used to date plantations. Plantations that were constructed from the end of the Revolutionary War until the opening shots of the Civil War are known as antebellum or "pre-war" plantations. Plantations that were built after the beginning of the Civil War are referred to as postbellum or "post-war" plantations. Postbellum plantations were also known as Reconstructionist plantations because they were constructed during the Reconstruction period following the Civil War.

ARCHITECTURAL DESIGNS

Although there are only two time periods during which plantations were constructed, there are several architectural styles that were used. The most common architectural designs used in the construction of the plantation houses include the Greek Revival, Georgian, Italianate/Italian Villa, Federal/Adam, Tidewater, Carpenter Gothic Revival, and Jeffersonian. Each has its own unique attributes that separates it from the others.

Carpenter Gothic Revival

The Carpenter Gothic design was popular in both the North and the South in the mid to late 1800s. Buildings constructed in this design often had physical characteristics similar to the gothic churches and other buildings that were popular in Europe until the 1600s.

One of the most distinguishing features of a Carpenter Gothic building is the very steep arches placed above the windows. The windows themselves are not usually rectangular, but are curved to be congruent with the arches constructed above. The roofs are usually arched as well, often extending several inches past the walls of the building itself.

Another sign that a building is Carpenter Gothic is the presence of one or more tall towers, usually on the corners of the main building. In a private house or cottage, the tower would likely be a sitting room or bedroom, whereas the tower of a Carpenter Gothic church often housed the church bell.

Although the Carpenter Gothic design adopted some characteristics from traditional Gothic architecture, there is one major difference between the two styles. Whereas the Gothic buildings were very elaborate in design, their Carpenter Gothic counterparts had a much more conservative appearance.

Most examples of Carpenter Gothic architecture can be found in smaller houses and churches. Although some plantation owners constructed their mansions in this style, most who used this design limited it to secondary buildings on the grounds or cottages or retreats far away from the plantation itself.

Italiante/Italian Villa

The Italian Villa style is loosely based on many of the homes and buildings found throughout the countryside of Italy, hence the name. The Italiante design became very popular in England in the 1840s and within a decade, houses and mansions were being built in America.

Most of the Italian Villa houses and mansions found in the South were constructed in the mid-1800s, shortly before and after the outbreak of the Civil War. Although many plantations in the Southern states were built in this style, most examples of Italian Villa homes can be found in the Northern states.

Like many other architectural styles, Italiante mansions and buildings often had one or more towers attached to the main structure. These towers were very square or rectangular and had a very distinct cornice, or decorative molding, surrounding the entire top. The roofs of the Italiante buildings often had a cornice covering the top edge of the entire building.

Whereas most buildings in other architectural styles are symmetrical, Italiante houses were often asymmetrical. It was not uncommon for the floorplan of an Italiante building to be in a "T" or "L."

Greek Revival

This architectural style was common among planters between 1800 and 1855. Greek Revival structures can be identified by the square or rounded columns that line the front of the building. Another feature of the Greek Revival plantation house is that there is often an oval window placed above the main entrance. A large number of state and federal government buildings are constructed using the Greek Revival architectural design.

Georgian

The Georgian architectural style was commonly used by planters between 1720 and 1840. It is very similar to the Greek Revival style, the main exception being that there is not an oval window installed above the main entrance. Georgian architecture heavily influenced the Greek Revival and Federal architectural styles.

Federal/Adam

Federal plantation mansions (also known as Adam style) were commonly built between the 1780s and the 1830s. The main difference between the Federal/Adam style and the Georgian or Greek Revival architectural styles is that the Federal plantation houses often have oval-shaped rooms. One of the most famous examples of this is the Oval Office of the White House.

Tidewater

The Tidewater architectural design was very popular among plantation owners near coastal areas throughout the early to mid-1800s. Tidewater houses can be identified by a wraparound porch that encompasses the entire structure. None of the other architectural designs have this feature. Another distinguishing characteristic of a Tidewater house is that the porches are slanted in order to protect the owners from rainstorms that are common along the coasts. The wraparound porches are also helpful in providing shade during the hottest days of the summer.

Jeffersonian

The Jeffersonian architectural style was used frequently between the 1790s and 1830s by some plantation owners. The Jeffersonian architectural style can easily be identified because the house has a round or octagonal shape, whereas the other plantation designs are either rectangular or square in shape.

Combination

Some plantation houses were built by utilizing features from more than one architectural style. There are a number of reasons that a combination plantation house was built. Rather than ordering expensive materials, many planters used materials found on the property. Some planters made bricks from the clay they found on the land. Those who owned coastal plantations would often use tabby, a type of cement made from seashells, limestone, and other ingredients.

A combination mansion was sometimes built because of the outbreak of the Civil War. Many times, an architect left a plantation house unfinished and returned to their home state. Rather than leaving the unfinished building to the elements, a planter had to improvise to save their house. Or, if a plantation house was acquired by another party, such as a descendant or buyer, modifications may have been made to suit their particular tastes.

GHOSTS AND HAUNTINGS ASSOCIATED WITH PLANTATIONS

Ghost stories and legends are often based on real events that occurred at some point in the past. If one should happen to experience a haunting, it is just as important to know the history of a location as it is to record a fascinating EVP or to capture an orb or apparition on film.

With enough research, a person can learn the *true facts* of a location that is reportedly haunted. This can only increase the person's understanding and appreciation of the plantation as well as give them a better grasp of *how* or *why* a place became haunted.

Not all plantations are reportedly haunted. Does this take away from the historical significance of a plantation? Not in the least. If you decide to visit haunted locations mentioned in this book or elsewhere, take some time to see locations that are not reportedly haunted. These places may give you a better idea of how life was during a particular historical period, which can be beneficial to having a better understanding of a place that *is* haunted.

There are certain conditions that need be present in order for a location to become haunted. These conditions are often found in abundance on and near plantations, and they include an emotional connection to a location, a sudden or violent death, or unfinished business. Considering the history between the planters, slaves, and soldiers often associated with a plantation, it is fairly easy to see that many plantations meet this criteria.

Generally a plantation is haunted by the ghosts of the plantation owner and family members, slaves, or Civil War soldiers. Below are a few examples of how each of these groups can meet the three criteria that can lead to a haunting.

There is often a great emotional connection associated with a plantation.

Plantation owners and their families often have a great sense of pride in their plantation. With the high mortality rate among plantation owners' children and other family members, the plantation house can also be a reminder of a loved one's death or serious illness.

Slaves that were on the plantation undoubtedly would have an emotional connection to the plantation. Virtually all of the slaves' morale was crushed by years of oppression and mistreatment by the plantation owners and their families. However, a few slaves developed strong feelings of affection toward the plantation owners and their families.

Union and Confederate soldiers who fought and died at the plantations would also have an emotional connection. Sometimes a battle
literally took place on the lawn in front of a plantation house. Other
times, a plantation house was taken over and used as a field hospital in
which several soldiers wounded in battle died.

There may have been a violent or sudden death that led to the haunting.

Between dying on the battlefield and less-than-ideal medical treatment, wounded Civil War soldiers are undoubtedly included in this
category.

There was a high mortality rate among plantation owners and their
families. Some women died in childbirth. Some plantation owners
were killed by another person in any of a variety of ways (poisoning,
shooting, duel, etc.). Some died from natural tragedies, such as drowning, house fires, and the like.

*Some places become haunted because an individual has unfinished busi-
ness and cannot rest until that business is completed.*

The children of plantation owners were sometimes forbidden to
marry a person they truly loved. Marriages were often arranged to
ensure that the children of plantation owners married people in their
own social class. This unrequited romance sometimes led to a person
literally grieving themselves to death or even committing suicide.

Sometimes a soldier made a promise to a loved one to return home
but died in war and was not able to do so. Hauntings have also included
a soldier so determined to carry out assigned duties that the apparitions
of guards standing at attention, or even providing medical service to
another soldier, have been seen.

I highly recommend that you who are involved in ghost hunting
do the investigation in a slow, methodical manner. It is important to
gather as much information as possible *before* visiting a haunted site.
Although paranormal investigations have gained a considerable following in recent years, it is important to present yourself in a professional
and respectful manner. While the technology outlined in my first book,

How to be a Ghost Hunter, may be obsolete, the core of the investigation protocol described in it is still solid.

A Word about Plantations Today

A number of plantations have been transformed into museums and state-run parks. There is more to a historical place than just a good ghost story. Take the time to learn from staff what the location has to offer in terms of historical significance.

The Kenworthy Hall/Carlisle-Martin House/Carlisle Hall Plantation, located in Marion, Alabama, is an Italian Villa style of architectural design. Courtesy Library of Congress.

Please keep in mind that many plantations are in fact private property and some of the owners are direct descendants or close family members of the original builders. If a plantation is on private property, please give the owners the privacy they deserve.

Some plantations listed in this book are now used as bed-and-breakfasts that cater to people from all walks of life. If you happen to stay at one of these bed-and-breakfasts, please be respectful and courteous of your hosts and any other guests who happen to be staying there as well. Sometimes these bed-and-breakfasts embrace reports of a haunting in order to add to the ambiance of their lodging. Others would rather not share that there are paranormal events that take place on the property.

Finally, some plantations have been abandoned for several years and are in a state of disrepair. While it may be exciting to go to an abandoned plantation house to ghost hunt, this may be very dangerous. There have been cases of abandoned but historically significant locations being completely destroyed by careless actions of people wanting to do a paranormal investigation.

In closing, I hope that you not only find enjoyment in reading about some of the legends and ghost stories of many of America's plantations, but I also hope that you may gain a better understanding of how plantations were significant in the formation of our country as it is today.

— TWO —

ALABAMA

CEDARHURST

Huntsville

Stephen Saunders Ewing moved to the Huntsville, Alabama, area in 1810 when he was only twenty-one years old. He purchased the first of many properties in the area two years later in 1812. Ewing married Mary Hutson Carter in 1814. Together they had a total of fourteen children, although a number of them did not survive into adulthood.

Ewing was pivotal in helping Huntsville become a prosperous Alabama community. He helped form the first bank in Huntsville and acted as bank president for several years. He was also actively involved in politics and held several local and regional offices while he lived in Huntsville.

In December 1823, Ewing purchased from Ebenezer Titus several hundred acres of property located near Huntsville, Alabama. Because of the number of cedar trees found on the property, Ewing decided to call his newest plantation Cedarhurst. After buying the land, Ewing cleared a great deal of the land and began to work on a plantation house. Construction of the mansion started in 1823 and was finally completed in 1825.

In early November 1837, Sally Carter, the fifteen-year-old younger sister of Mary Carter Ewing, came to Cedarhurst for a visit. While at

Cedarhurst, Sally became seriously ill and died a few days later, on November 28, 1837. After a small funeral service, Sally was buried in the Ewing family cemetery located near the plantation house.

Stephen continued to manage Cedarhurst until his wife's death in 1849. After her death, he could no longer stay at Cedarhurst and he put the property up for sale. In 1865, Ewing sold the entire plantation to Robert Brickwell. After Ewing sold Cedarhurst, he moved from Huntsville, Alabama, to Aberdeen, Mississippi, where he died in 1867 at age seventy-eight.

After Brickwell purchased the property in 1865, Cedarhurst Plantation was sold a total of five times until finally purchased by J.D. Thornton in 1919. It has been reported that shortly after Thornton moved in and started to make renovations on the mansion, the paranormal events began to occur.

The most notable appearance of Sally's ghost took place a few months after Thornton purchased Cedarhurst. During the summer of 1919, a teenage relative named Charles Rothan visited from out of town for a few days. One night, Rothan had a dream in which a beautiful teenage girl visited him. She told him that her name was Sally and that she died at Cedarhurst a long time ago and was buried in the family cemetery. Rothan claimed Sally told him that her gravestone had been toppled over during a thunderstorm and that she needed it returned to its upright position.

When Charles told his family the next morning, they went to the Ewing family graveyard and found that Sally's headstone had indeed been toppled to the ground. It is not known whether Charles helped Sally, but he soon left Cedarhurst and never visited the house again.

After word spread of Charles's encounter with Sally Carter's ghost, dozens of people visited her gravesite and claimed to have seen her apparition standing over her tombstone. The apparition seen at the gravesite is identical to an apparition seen in and near the bedroom where Sally Carter died in 1837.

Since 1985, the Cedarhurst Plantation House has been the central office of a private gated housing community. As it is a private housing community, visitors or passersby are not permitted on the property without permission.

When ground was broken to begin construction of the housing community in the early 1980s, the Ewing family graves at Cedarhurst were exhumed and reburied at nearby Maple Hill Cemetery. Out of respect, and because of the legends and stories that surround Sally's headstone, her remains were buried in an unmarked grave somewhere in the cemetery. It is uncertain if Sally's apparition still makes an appearance near where her original grave was, but there have been no reports of a ghost at all in the Maple Hill Cemetery.

Although her body was moved to Maple Hill Cemetery, Sally's apparition has continued to be seen in the bedroom in the Cedarhurst Plantation House where she died. In addition to the apparition, there have been accounts of occasional poltergeist activity in the mansion, including pillows and other small items being moved without explanation.

DR. JOHN R. DRISH HOUSE/ DRISH PLANTATION
Tuscaloosa

Dr. Jonathan R. Drish moved to the Tuscaloosa, Alabama, area from Louden County, Virginia, in 1822. Within a few years, Dr. Drish had established himself in the community as both a prominent physician and a building contractor.

In 1835, Drish married a local widow by the name of Sarah McKinney, and to commemorate their union Dr. Drish purchased a 450-acre tract on the outskirts of Tuscaloosa. Immediately, he began construction of a large two-story Italianate mansion designed by architect William Nichols. As was commonplace in the antebellum South, Drish's slaves provided labor for the mansion, which was completed two years later in 1837.

As soon as Nichols completed the mansion, Dr. Drish immediately began to make several modifications to the mansion's interior and exterior from 1837 until the outbreak of the Civil War in 1861. One of the most prominent modifications was the construction of a large three-story brick tower on the front of the mansion, which became the building's most prominent feature.

Dr. Drish died in 1867 from complications due to falling down a staircase inside the mansion. The viewing and funeral took place at the Drish Plantation House a few days later with family, friends, and other plantation owners coming from all over the state of Alabama to pay their final respects to Dr. Drish.

While Jonathan Drish's body lay in state, Sarah lit candles in honor of her husband and made certain that they remained lit next to her husband's body until the funeral services had been concluded. After the funeral service, Mrs. Drish extinguished the candles with the instruction that they were only to be lit again upon her own death.

A few years before her death in 1884, Mrs. Drish became increasingly obsessed with burning candles of all kinds. She would reportedly have dozens of candles burning in several rooms throughout the mansion at all hours of the day and night.

After Sarah Drish passed away, it was discovered by family members that she had not made out a will, or made any plans whatsoever as to what she wanted to do with the plantation. There was a great deal of confusion and debate in regards to how the estate would be divided and what would happen to the property. It was not known what Sarah's wishes were for her funeral, so her family had to improvise.

In making preparations for Sarah's funeral, one minor detail was overlooked. Seventeen years earlier, Sarah had requested that the candles that were lit next to her husband would be lit at her own viewing and funeral. The candles lay untouched and were not lit at her viewing, funeral, or at any time prior to her burial a few days later. After Sarah was buried, the mansion remained vacant for several years.

In 1906, Drish Mansion was purchased and used as a schoolhouse for nearly thirty years until it closed in 1935. In 1940, Drish Mansion was purchased by the Southside Baptist Church and was used as a church until the 1990s. After this, the mansion fell into a state of disrepair and was in danger of being lost until the property was purchased by Tuscaloosa County Preservation Society in 2007.

The vast majority of the paranormal activity associated with the Drish Mansion is centered around Sarah Drish and her candles.

A few months after Sarah Drish had been buried, the third-floor tower of Drish Mansion appeared to have caught fire, although nobody was living in the mansion at the time. The blaze was reportedly so bright that it could be seen for several miles. When neighbors and a local fire brigade approached the mansion, they found that the mansion was not on fire and that there was no sign that it had ever been on fire. Over the next few years, the fire appeared two or three more times. Each time the fire brigade and neighbors went to the mansion and found that there was no fire to put out.

After the third appearance, the fires stopped being seen. By this time, the Drish Mansion had the reputation of being haunted, and curious thrill seekers began to walk by the building. When this started, there were several accounts that the ghost of Sarah Drish was seen either in front of the mansion or looking out the third-story window of the tower, which was where the phantom fires had been seen.

When Drish Mansion was used as Jemison School in the early 1900s, the school's official stance was that no paranormal activity had ever taken place on the property. However, people who walked by the mansion claimed to have seen Sarah Drish's ghost sitting in the third-floor window of the tower.

After the school closed in 1935, and long after it was purchased by the Southside Baptist Church, there were reports of floating lights, often described as candlelight, through the windows of the entire mansion. It is believed that the light is coming from candles that Sarah Drish lit in memory of her husband.

FORKS OF CYPRESS

Florence

James Jackson, an immigrant from Ballybay, Ireland, moved to Florence, Alabama, in the spring of 1818. Two years later, Jackson hired architect William Nicholson to design the large Greek Revival-style mansion and other outbuildings on the plantation. Construction started in the early 1820s and was completed nearly a decade later in 1830. Jackson named the plantation Forks of Cypress because the Little Cypress Creek and the Big Cypress Creek merged near where the plantation house was built.

James Jackson was renowned for his ability to breed the finest thoroughbred racing horses in the nation. From the time he settled in Florence, Alabama, in 1818 through the early 1830s, Jackson arranged to have more than a dozen English thoroughbred horses shipped to Forks of Cypress. Their offspring were largely sought after by the wealthiest plantation owners and politicians in the nation.

James Jackson died on August 17, 1840, and is buried in the family cemetery near the main plantation house. His widow, Sarah "Sally" Moore Jackson, inherited the property and took over all of the work associated with its upkeep, including the continuation of breeding his prized Kentucky thoroughbreds. During the Civil War, Forks of Cypress was used by Union troops as a base camp for several hundred troops.

The original mansion was struck by lightning and burned to the ground on June 6, 1966. Although the mansion was completely destroyed, most of the brick pillars remain standing to this day. The brick columns are likely still standing because they were covered in a layer of plaster that contained horse hair, which acted as a fire retardant. Today, the Forks of Cypress is open to the public and the ruins can be toured throughout the year.

There have been accounts of ghostly activity taking place at the Forks of Cypress Plantation House since long before the mansion's destruction in 1966. According to legend, a reporter who was a guest at the plantation house a few days before it burned had trouble sleeping. He blamed his insomnia on the sounds of gunfire, footsteps, and a scream heard throughout the night. It is possible that the reporter might to have heard the ghosts of the Union soldiers who used the plantation as a base camp. To this day, there have been reports of similar phenomena as what the reporter claimed when he stayed at the mansion.

In regards to the Jackson family graveyard, since the 1930s there has been a ghost story about an apparition of a tall, thin woman walking among the headstones. The Jackson family graveyard is surrounded by a wrought-iron fence approximately ten feet high, so the possibility of climbing the fence or getting past the locked gate is unlikely. Although not confirmed, most people believe the apparition is that of James Jackson's wife, Sarah Jackson.

Another graveyard at Forks of Cypress that is said to be haunted is the nearby slave graveyard. This graveyard is not surrounded by a fence, but very few people visit it. Paranormal investigators who have visited the slave graveyard claim to have recorded EVPs of people crying. In addition, an African American spiritual has been heard being sung from within the cemetery.

Finally, the ghost of an African American man can be seen walking away from the Forks of Cypress Mansion. Sometimes slaves were given permission to visit family who lived at neighboring plantations. It is believed that this man is walking toward another plantation not far from the Forks of Cypress to meet his wife.

GAINESWOOD

Demopolis

General Nathan Bryan Whitfield was a cotton planter from North Carolina who moved to Demopolis, Alabama, in 1834. In 1842, Whitfield bought a 480-acre plantation from George Gaines, who had built a modest yet comfortable log house for his family. When Whitfield moved onto the property, he lived in the log home for a year while he built several rooms, which were connected to the existing building.

Beginning in 1843, Whitfield spent nearly twenty years making renovations to the cabin that transformed it into a majestic Greek Revival mansion. Ironically, Whitfield completed the renovations to the mansion on April 11, 1861, only one day prior to the official outbreak of the Civil War. Several outbuildings, including slave quarters and a detached kitchen, were constructed near the main mansion. Upon completion of the mansion and surrounding outbuildings, General Whitfield christened the plantation Gaineswood in honor of George Gaines, the original owner of the property.

The one architectural marvel that makes Gaineswood Plantation stand out from other plantations is a drainage ditch that Whitfield had constructed near the house. Due to its location, the plantation house and surrounding property was in constant danger of being flooded each spring by the heavy rains common in this area of the country.

Whitfield used slave labor to have a one-mile drainage ditch built from near the plantation house to the Tombigbee River. Construction of the ditch started in 1845 and took nearly twenty years to complete. Throughout the project, the slaves had a difficult time digging the drainage ditch by hand because they often encountered hard clay, which in some areas reached a depth of between twenty-five and thirty feet.

General Whitfield's wife, Elizabeth, died in 1846. After her death, Whitfield was unable to raise his children by himself because of his many business obligations abroad. After weeks of searching, Whitfield found and hired Evelyn Carter to become a live-in caretaker and nanny for his children. Evelyn developed a strong rapport with Whitfield and his two children. Soon, Whitfield felt comfortable enough to resume his business travel knowing that the children were well taken care of.

One winter a few years after she was hired, Evelyn contracted pneumonia. Although Whitfield arranged for Evelyn to be given the best medical care possible, her symptoms worsened and she realized that she was likely going to die. On her deathbed, Evelyn made Whitfield promise to have her body moved to Virginia to be buried in her family cemetery. Whitfield assured her that he would make certain that her final request was honored. Although Whitfield and his children hoped that Evelyn would recover, she passed away a few days later.

Unfortunately, the winter had been harsh and the severe weather prevented Evelyn's body from being moved several hundred miles north before it would have started to decompose. General Whitfield had little choice but to break his promise to Evelyn and bury her in his family cemetery at the plantation. He had every intention of exhuming her body the following spring and transporting it to Virginia for burial. Whitfield also knew that Evelyn desperately wanted her father to attend her funeral, but he was in Greece at the time of her death. Whitfield thought that if Evelyn's funeral was conducted the following spring in Virginia, he would have fulfilled at least this small request.

Evelyn's death was not the only tragedy that General Whitfield experienced at Gaineswood. Early on the morning of March 1, 1858, one of the most horrific ship disasters in Alabama's history took place on the Tombigbee River very close to the Gainesville Plantation. A cargo and passenger riverboat called the *Eliza Battle* launched from Columbus, Alabama, with scheduled stops in Gainesville and Demopolis, Alabama.

The *Eliza Battle* had made the trip up and down the Tombigbee River without incident and the crew was very familiar with the route. On this particular trip, the *Eliza Battle* carried over one thousand bales of cotton, forty-five crew members, and approximately fifty-five passengers.

Around 2:00 a.m., a fire broke out among the dry bales of cotton, accidentally set by a crewman who started a small fire to stay warm in the thirty-degree weather. It is believed that a stray spark or ember landed on the dry cotton and ignited it. Most of the passengers were asleep and were unaware of the fire until the entire ship was completely engulfed in flames. To save as many passengers as he could, Captain

Graham Stone tried to steer the burning *Eliza Battle* as close to shore as possible. The closest landing to the *Eliza Battle* was Kemp's Landing, near the Gaineswood Plantation.

Whitfield was awakened by a house servant who had seen the fire on the river. The plantation house was about one mile from the Tombigbee River, but Whitfield could still see the flames and hear the screams from the *Eliza Battle*. It was later told by survivors that some passengers had to choose drowning in freezing water or burning to death on the blazing riverboat. The vision remained with Whitfield for the remainder of his life and was the inspiration of "The Burning of the *Eliza Battle*," a painting that is still on display at Gaineswood Plantation.

Between the *Eliza Battle* fire, Evelyn's death, and the hard work associated with the drainage ditch, Gaineswood may very well be one of most haunted plantations in the state of Alabama. There have been ghost stories associated with each of these different parts of Gaineswood's history.

One ghost connected with Gaineswood is that of General Whitfield. In the room that used to be his study, visitors to Gaineswood have noticed the strong aroma of pipe tobacco. It was known that Whitfield would often smoke a pipe in this room when he was working, and the smell of tobacco smoke is believed to be a testament to that. Although there have been paranormal investigations in this room in the past, other than the scent of pipe tobacco, there have not been any apparitions or other ghostly activities associated with this room.

There are two separate areas of the mansion that are reportedly haunted by Evelyn Carter's ghost. On the main steps or near the birthing room on the second floor, a woman has been seen making her rounds as if she is checking out the room. People who walk past the birthing room have felt a sensation of being lightly pushed. It is believed that this is the ghost of Evelyn Carter, because it was well known that she checked on the children several times each night after they went to sleep.

The second room is the music room on the first floor, where Evelyn could often be found playing the piano. The sound of a person playing classical pieces on the piano has been heard in this room.

The mile-long drainage ditch from the Gaineswood Plantation House to the Tombigbee River has also been rumored to be a hot spot of paranormal activity. The sounds of digging and voices in conversation have been reported and are believed to be from the ghosts of slaves who spent twenty years digging the mile-long drainage ditch.

The final haunting connected to Gaineswood Plantation is not on the plantation itself, but on the nearby Tombigbee River. On certain nights, the *Eliza Battle* can still be seen on the Tombigbee River. Eyewitnesses have claimed to have seen a large, burning riverboat engulfed in flames. This apparition is often accompanied by the smell of burning wood and the screams of the passengers and crew members. River men who still travel the Tombigbee River claim that if the ghost ship of the *Eliza Battle* is seen, it is a warning that a disaster or tragedy will take place in the near future.

KENWORTHY HALL/CARLISLE-MARTIN HOUSE/ CARLISLE HALL

Marion

Edward Kenworthy Carlisle was born in 1810 near Augusta, Georgia. As a teenager, Carlisle moved to Marion, Alabama, to help work the cotton fields with his mother's family, who owned property in the area. Carlisle settled near Marion and saved all of the money he had made from working for his mother's family. In less than ten years, he had made quite a living for himself and purchased 440 acres to establish a cotton plantation of his own.

In 1843, Carlisle married Lucinda Wilson Walthall. The couple had two children, Edward Jr. and Anne. In order to provide a comfortable household for his family, Carlisle constructed an elaborate Italian Villa-style mansion, built between 1858 and 1860, on his 440-acre plantation. When building the mansion, Carlisle spared no expense, which was evident in that many of the materials used to build the mansion were imported from Europe.

Carlisle spent a great deal of his money on the mansion, but a few years after the end of the Civil War, his estimated net worth was only between $15,000 and $20,000. The 440 acres, including the mansion, was estimated to be worth only about $9,000. This was only a small fraction of what Carlisle had invested into its construction.

When Carlisle's daughter, Anne, was a teenager, she met and fell in love with the son of another plantation owner. However, the Civil War broke out and Anne's beau enlisted in the Confederate army. Before he left, he proposed to Anne and she accepted. She promised her new fiancé that she would look out the fourth-floor window of the plantation's tower and pray for his safe return.

After hearing nothing from him for several weeks, Anne began to worry and spent more time isolated in the tower. One day, she saw a servant from her fiancé's plantation approaching on foot. She rushed down to see the servant, who informed her that her fiancé was killed in a battle and was buried near where he died. It was not uncommon for soldiers killed in action to be buried near where they died rather than being sent home to be buried.

Anne fell into a deep depression and isolated herself on the fourth floor of the mansion's tower. Within a few months, Anne died. Immediately after Anne's death, her apparition began to be seen in the tower. Her ghost is often accompanied by the sound of crying and the faint smell of sweet perfume. Sometimes, people who have encountered Anne's ghost claim to have also encountered a strong sense of sadness.

ROCKY HILL CASTLE/ROCKY HILL
Rocky Hill

James Saunders wanted to make a name for himself. Instead of simply inheriting Saunders Hall Plantation from his father, Turner Saunders, James purchased 640 acres a few miles from Saunders Hall. He moved to the property shortly after he met and married Mary Francis Watkins in July 1824 at eighteen years of age. Within a few years after moving into a small home on the property, James Saunders became known as both a plantation owner and a successful attorney.

In the mid-1850s, Saunders tore down the small house that he and his wife had lived in and constructed a large mansion built on a hill toward the center of his property. He hired a renowned French architect to construct a mansion for him with orders that it be one of the most beautiful mansions in the area. Although the mansion was a combination of the Greek Revival and Italianate architectural styles, one feature added was a five-story Gothic Revival tower built onto its western side. This particular tower is what gave the mansion its unique appearance and ultimately the name of Rocky Hill Castle.

Ground was broken for the mansion in 1858 and was nearly completed in 1861 when the Civil War began. The French architect stopped working on the plantation and left the area. Some believe that the architect was a Union sympathizer, while others believe that Saunders simply ran out of money and was unable to pay him. In either case, the architect left Rocky Hill Castle unfinished and departed the area just as Union troops reached the plantation.

Noticing what was starting to happen to the entire nation as Union and Confederate soldiers began to fight, Saunders took his family and left the unfinished mansion. After Saunders left Rocky Hill Castle, the mansion was commandeered by Confederate officers and transformed into a field hospital for wounded soldiers. Although Rocky Hill Castle had been spared, most of Saunders's personal belongings were completely destroyed.

Due to the large number of soldiers treated at Rocky Hill in less-than-ideal conditions, the fatality rate was very high. It is believed that a large number of Confederate casualties may lie buried in unmarked graves on the property, some of which have not been found to this day.

After the war ended, James Saunders and his family returned to Rocky Hill Castle and began to repair the heavily damaged mansion.

The property stayed in the Saunders family until the mid-1920s, when it was acquired by James Saunders's grandson, Dr. Dudley Saunders. Dr. Saunders did not stay at the mansion long before he decided to sell the property. Some sources state that Dr. Saunders and his family left and ultimately sold the property after experiencing a variety of paranormal activity. After Dr. Saunders moved from the mansion, it was abandoned and left to the elements for several years.

Due to Rocky Hill Castle being vacant from the 1920s until the early 1960s, it was apparent that no amount of renovation could restore the house to its original condition. Shortly after it was purchased again in 1961, the plantation house and surrounding buildings were torn down and the ground was leveled. All that is left of Rocky Hill Castle today are photographs and documents associated with the mansion.

The hauntings of the plantation house date back to when the Saunders family returned to Rocky Hill during the Reconstruction period after the Civil War. Mary Saunders herself was reportedly one of the first people to have had a paranormal encounter shortly after returning to Rocky Hill. She was near the main entryway on the first floor of the mansion and noticed a young woman wearing a blue dress standing on the main stairway. When she approached the young woman to ask her what business she had in her home, the woman disappeared before her eyes. Mrs. Saunders mentioned her experience to her family, who initially did not believe her. However, over the next several months, other family members and visitors saw the apparition, which eventually became known as the Lady in Blue.

The Lady in Blue has been described as a young woman with shoulder-length brown hair and wearing a light blue dress. She appears to be oblivious to her surroundings; she does not seem to be aware of any eyewitnesses who have attempted to communicate with her over the last several years. The Lady in Blue can be seen walking in the Saunders family cemetery as if she was searching for something.

The identity of the Lady in Blue was never discovered, although some think that the ghost is of a nurse who assisted wounded soldiers when Rocky Hill was a Confederate field hospital. It is also possible that the Lady in Blue was a loved one of a Confederate soldier who died at the mansion.

Another ghost that allegedly haunts the area where Rocky Hill Castle stood is that of the French architect who designed the mansion. It is believed that he died shortly after leaving the plantation house and that his ghost still haunts the area. Until it was demolished in 1961, the sound of hammering was heard at all hours of the night. Some believe that the sound of construction was of the French architect or the slaves used to build the mansion.

Apparitions of Confederate soldiers have been seen in front of where the mansion stood and at the Saunders family cemetery. Sometimes the medical staff was so busy taking care of wounded soldiers that the dead and dying were unceremoniously buried in shallow, unmarked graves close to the mansion. There have also been the reports of the sounds of gunfire immediately followed by the sounds of screaming or moaning that cease after a few seconds.

A number of slave quarters were built not far from the main mansion on the plantation. Paranormal investigators and other eyewitnesses over the years have reported hearing the sounds of hushed voices that suddenly stop as a person approaches near where the cabins once stood. The sounds of screaming and crying have also been heard in this area, but it is uncertain whether the sounds are coming from the ghosts of the slaves or of the soldiers who died on the plantation. In addition, the smell of cooking food has been noticed near where the slave cabins once stood.

SPRING VILLA
Opelika

Arthur Yonge immigrated to the United States from Europe in 1812. Starting in Florida, Arthur Yonge moved a few times before finally settling in Georgia. There, Arthur made a fairly comfortable living for his family, which included his wife and his son, William Penn Chandler Yonge.

William was born in 1822. Arthur Yonge died when William was twelve years old and left him absolutely nothing as an inheritance. After Arthur Yonge's death, it is uncertain what became of William's mother and siblings. However, destitute and literally abandoned by his family, William was forced to fend for himself from the time he was twelve years old until he reached adulthood. Believing that Georgia had little to offer him, William Yonge soon moved to Alabama, where nobody knew of his past or his name.

Through his teenage years, William took care of himself by working at a variety of jobs. He realized that appearance and attitude made all the difference in making a lasting impression to business associates. By his early twenties, Yonge had established himself as a very savvy businessman. He gave the air of confidence of a formally educated man, though very few knew of his meager background.

When Yonge was twenty-four years old, he met and married Alabama native Mary Ann Godwin. The trust that the two had for one another was crucial because work often required William to be away from his wife for months on end. During the California Gold Rush in 1849, William spent eighteen months in California. When he returned to Alabama in 1851, William had acquired a considerable fortune from his hard work.

Using money from his trip to California, Yonge purchased a large tract of land near Opelika, Alabama. On the property, Yonge commissioned the construction of a large Carpenter Gothic Revival mansion that overlooked a beautiful thirty-acre lake. Because of the proximity of the mansion to the lake, Yonge named his plantation Spring Villa. Today, it is one of the few examples of Gothic Revival architecture still standing in Alabama.

Not long after returning to Alabama in 1851, Yonge started to make preparations for another trip to California to find more gold. However, he discovered that some property close to where he lived had large deposits of natural lime. He purchased the property with the funds he was going to use to return to California. Excavating the lime near his own home was more profitable and less expensive than another trip to California. Once he owned the property, Yonge began to excavate the lime, which was in great demand by many local businesses.

During the Civil War, Yonge remained financially secure, as much of the lime was used to build fortifications for the Confederate army to keep the Union troops at bay. During the economic collapse of the Confederate States of America at the end of the Civil War, Yonge lost a great deal of his fortune. Yonge died in 1879 with only a fraction of the money that he had made during his years selling lime.

It is uncertain exactly how William Yonge died, although records do indicate that he died in 1879. One legend surrounding his death is that a disgruntled servant hid in the shadows of the spiral staircases that led to Yonge's bedroom on the second floor. After everybody except for Yonge was asleep, the servant crept up behind him on the staircase and stabbed him to death. Although the identity of the killer remains a mystery, some also speculate that it may have been a robber or one of his former slaves who returned to stab Yonge.

Today, the mansion is located on a 325-acre state park with hiking trails, campsites, picnic areas, and other amenities for the public. The plantation house, campground, and shelter can be reserved for special occasions.

The area of the Spring Villa Plantation House believed to be haunted is at the top of the staircase where Yonge was stabbed. In this area, a shadowy figure has been seen and photographed, and there have also been reports of the sound of a struggle on the steps, although when it is investigated, there is no sign that anybody has been on the staircase at all.

At least one paranormal group was able to record a very impressive EVP in a second-floor bedroom of the mansion. The EVP is of a little girl who asks the question, "Can you see me?" This voice was not heard when the room was investigated, but only after the audio recording was played. The identity of the little girl is not known; there have been no reports of a girl who died in the plantation house.

STURDIVANT MANSION/ WATTS-PARKMAN-GILLMAN HOME
Selma

In 1852, plantation owner Colonel Edward Watts commissioned renowned architect Thomas Helm Lee to design and supervise construction of a Greek Revival mansion that would become known as Sturdivant Hall or Sturdivant Mansion. Construction commenced in 1852 and was completed four years later in 1856. Immediately after the mansion was completed, Edward Watts and his family moved in.

The Civil War caused considerable financial hardship for the Watts family. On February 12, 1862, Watts sold the mansion and surrounding property to a local banker by the name of John McGee Parkman for $65,000 cash. Once the property was sold, Watts relocated his family to Texas. Realizing that the value of cash he received would likely depreciate due to the Civil War, he immediately used the money to purchase a large piece of property in Texas. When Watts and his family vacated the premises, Parkman immediately moved in.

After the Civil War ended, Parkman became president of the First National Bank of Selma, Alabama. Although he was elated with the promotion, it would eventually lead to Parkman's ultimate undoing. The bank offered risky, high-interest loans to planters to help rebuild their plantations. Parkman hoped that he could make money from their misfortune. However, many planters were unable to make their payments and the First National Bank of Selma experienced considerable financial losses and was in danger of closing. It was speculated that in order to save himself, Parkman embezzled large sums of money, because he feared that the bank would be closed.

When word got out of Parkman's apparent embezzlement, it caught the attention of Wager Swayne, acting military governor of Alabama during the Reconstruction period. Parkman was arrested and imprisoned at Castle Morgan, a Confederate prisoner-of-war camp located in Cahaba, Alabama. Throughout his incarceration, Parkman proclaimed his innocence and was adamant that he had been framed. He said that he would never leave Selma until his name was cleared. Although he loudly claimed his innocence, shortly after he was incarcerated Parkman was killed on May 23, 1867 during an escape attempt.

After Parkman's death, the mansion was vacant for three years until it was purchased in January 1870 by merchant Robert Sturdivant. The property stayed in the Sturdivant family until the late 1950s, when it was sold to the city of Selma, Alabama, for $75,000. The family of Robert Sturdivant donated $50,000 to the city for the purchase of the mansion with the condition that it be renovated into a museum and named after him.

The most prominent ghost associated with Sturdivant Mansion is that of the second owner of the mansion, John Parkman. A great deal of Parkman's story and related hauntings can be found in Kathryn Windham's book, *13 Alabama Ghosts and Jeffrey.*

Since the time Sturdivant Hall became a museum that was open to the public, Parkman's ghost has been seen inside the mansion on several occasions. Generally, the haunting consists of poltergeist activity in two of the rooms on the first floor. However, visitors to the plantation house have photographed ghostly images of an apparition fitting Parkman's description standing near the main entrance of Sturdivant Hall.

There are two possible reasons that Sturdivant Hall may be haunted by Parkman's ghost. Before his death, Parkman claimed that he was not guilty of embezzlement and would not rest until his name was cleared. Another legend associated with the mansion claims that shortly before he was arrested, Parkman hid away a large portion of the money that he was believed to have embezzled.

SWEETWATER PLANTATION
Florence

The Sweetwater Plantation is one of the oldest plantation houses in Alabama. It was designed by General John Brahan, a veteran of the War of 1812 and a member of the Alabama Militia. Brahan was born in 1774 in Virginia and moved to Florence, Alabama, in 1818 with his wife. After settling in Florence, Brahan purchased approximately 4,000 acres outside of the town.

In addition to maintaining Sweetwater Plantation, Brahan became a very well-known fixture in the area because of his involvement in founding the Nativity Episcopal Church in Huntsville, Alabama, as well as his generosity to the city of Florence, Alabama, and his active participation in a local Masonic lodge.

Construction of the mansion began in 1828, but General Brahan died on June 8, 1834, only a year before the mansion was completed. Upon General Brahan's death, his son-in-law, Robert Patton, took over the construction of the mansion, which was completed the following year in 1835. Patton named the plantation Sweetwater because Sweetwater Creek ran through the property near the mansion's building site. Robert Patton would become Alabama's twentieth governor, serving from 1865 to 1867.

The mansion was exceptional for a number of reasons. The bricks used to build Sweetwater Mansion were made on site by Brahan's slaves. Using clay found on the property to make the bricks cut the cost of the construction of the mansion considerably and allowed Brahan the opportunity to spend money on other details of the mansion, such as importing marble from Italy and wood from England.

Over the course of several years, Sweetwater Plantation gained the reputation of being haunted by many of the people who lived on the property at one time or another. The sound of children playing and laughing can be heard throughout the mansion. It is likely that the children were those of John Brahan. In addition to these sounds, there

have been some reports of poltergeist activity and electrical disturbances on the second floor. Water faucets in the mansion have been
turned on by an unseen presence. Finally, the sound of a piano playing
has actually been recorded in an empty room on the first floor.

Although these experiences can be considered very interesting in
and of themselves, the most pronounced haunting reported at the
Sweetwater Mansion is focused in one of the sitting rooms on the first
floor. At the outset of the Civil War, one of Governor Patton's sons
decided to volunteer his services for the Confederate army. Shortly after enlisting, Patton's son was killed in action not far from Sweetwater
Plantation. The body of General Patton's son was returned to Sweetwater, where a funeral was held in the sitting room on the first floor.

Since his death, the apparition of what appears to be a casket has
been seen by dozens of eyewitnesses. One of the most detailed descriptions of the apparition comes from a mansion caretaker who had
seen the phantom casket. Rather than being frightened, the man was
curious enough to walk up to the casket and look inside. Lying inside
the casket was a man in a Confederate uniform. At that point, the apparition disappeared.

The hauntings associated with Sweetwater Plantation caught the
attention of the producers of *Paranormal State*, which featured Sweetwater Plantation in an episode called "Southern Discomfort" that originally aired in April 2011 on the A&E Network.

— THREE —

GEORGIA

ANTEBELLUM PLANTATION
Stone Mountain

Rather than a single plantation house constructed by a single plant-er, the buildings of Antebellum Plantation at Stone Mountain Park are actually a collection of structures that give visitors a glimpse of what nineteenth century plantation life was like. All of the buildings of Antebellum Plantation were constructed between 1790 and 1845 and were found at various locations throughout Georgia. Once State Mountain Park was opened, the buildings were carefully transport-ed to the site, where they have been standing to this day.

Three of the more prominent structures at Antebellum Plantation are believed to be haunted by former residents who lived in the build-ings before they were moved to Stone Mountain Park. This gives cre-dence to the fact that in some cases a ghost haunts a building rather than a piece of property; if ghosts were attached to the original land rather than the buildings, there would be no hauntings in the buildings that were moved to Stone Mountain Park.

The most haunted building at Antebellum Plantation is believed to be the Thornton House, which was originally located in Union Point, Georgia. It is also the oldest building at Antebellum Plantation, being constructed in 1790, and is perhaps the best preserved example of this type of antebellum architecture in the entire state.

The ghost associated with the Thornton House is of an unidentified boy about ten or eleven years old. He is described as having blond hair and brown eyes and wearing a long-sleeved shirt and long pants with suspenders. He has always been seen on the second floor of the mansion near a bedroom that was used by the original owner's son.

Another haunted building at Antebellum Plantation is the Dickey House. This plantation house was originally constructed in 1840 near Dickey, Georgia. Although it lay abandoned for several years before it was relocated, the Dickey House was chosen to be on display at Stone Mountain Park because of its good physical condition.

Unlike the Thornton House where there have been close-up experiences with the boy's apparition, the ghost at the Dickey House is always seen from a distance. This ghost is that of a young dark-haired woman who appears in the top-floor window of the mansion. Initially, visitors who saw the woman believed that she was a Civil War re-enactor or a staff member. However, when repeated searches of the mansion found nothing, it became apparent that the woman was actually the ghost of somebody associated with the original mansion. The dark-haired woman is described as sad or depressed and is always seen looking from the window onto the lawn in front of the mansion.

The third location believed to be haunted at Antebellum Plantation is two slave cabins that were originally part of Graves Plantation in Covington, Georgia. These two cabins were constructed in 1830 by slaves who lived in them for several years. The paranormal activity connected to the slave cabins includes an overwhelming sensation of oppression and of being watched, an occasional and noticeable drop in temperature, and the faint sounds of voices in hushed conversation or singing.

BARNSLEY GARDENS/ADAIR HOUSE
Adairsville

Godfrey Barnsley emigrated from England in 1823 when he was only eighteen years old. Approximately six years after settling in Georgia, he found a job at a warehouse that shipped cotton to all parts of the nation. Through hard work and dedication, Barnsley developed a reputation for being a very ambitious and astute employee.

By saving his earnings from working at the warehouse and by making wise business investments, Godfrey owned over 10,000 acres by the time he met Julia Scarborough. After a fairly short courtship, he and Julia were married on December 24, 1828. When they were married, he and Julia moved to one of his plantations and planned the construction of a large mansion that was going to be a combination of Italianate Villa and Gothic Revival designs. As the plans for the plantation began to materialize and even before construction of the mansion commenced, Godfrey and Julia referred to this property as the Woodlands.

Before Godfrey broke ground on the mansion at the Woodlands, he was approached by a close friend of Cherokee descent. Godfrey excitedly shared his plans to build a mansion on a particular area on his property, but was informed by his friend that the land was sacred to the Cherokee and desecrating it in any way would cause misery and tragedy for the person responsible for its desecration. Godfrey felt that his friend was superstitious and ignored the warning about building the mansion. When Godfrey broke ground, his friend never spoke to him again.

Godfrey wanted to have an elaborate botanical garden built to compliment the mansion. The garden was completed before the mansion and Godfrey and Julia spent hours walking through it. The botanical garden was so beautiful that soon the property became known as Barnsley Gardens.

Construction of the mansion began in late 1841 or early 1842 and was nearly completed by early 1845. Although not quite finished, Godfrey and his family moved into a section of the mansion that was completed. A few months after moving in, Godfrey's wife, Julia, contracted tuberculosis and died in the summer of 1845. Without the support of his wife, Godfrey ceased construction of the mansion for a few years. Before he was able to resume the building of the plantation house, one of his young daughters died in 1848 after a short illness.

Godfrey went into a deep depression and had given up on not only finishing the mansion, but also on his career. He spent hours walking through the elaborate botanical garden that he built for his wife near the mansion. One day while walking through the garden, Godfrey claimed to have had a visitation from the spirit of his deceased wife. She told him that she loved him and wanted him to complete the mansion, which was a testament of their love. After his experience with Julia's ghost, Godfrey immediately resumed work with a renewed vigor and made the necessary arrangements to finish the mansion as quickly as possible. The mansion was finally completed by the end of 1848.

Godfrey remained at the Woodlands into the mid-1860s. Although he was greatly interested in the outcome of the Civil War and was a Southern sympathizer, he really did not want to become too involved with the conflicts associated with it. However, that mindset changed in May 1864 when a ground battle between Union and Confederate cavalries was fought on Godfrey's property.

Colonel R.G. Earle of the second Alabama Light Calvary was a close friend of Godfrey's and broke rank to warn him to leave the Woodlands before the battle reached the plantation house. Before Earle could reach Godfrey, he was shot five times by Union troops and was killed in the botanical garden in front of the mansion. The Union troops overtook the Confederates near the plantation house. After the battle, Union soldiers entered the mansion and destroyed most of Godfrey's furnishings and other belongings.

After the Civil War ended, Godfrey lost all of his fortune because Confederate money was no longer of value. Penniless, he moved to New Orleans and died there in 1873. After Godfrey's death, his body was returned to the family graveyard at the plantation.

With such an emotional connection to the plantation, it makes sense that Godfrey Barnsley's ghost would haunt Barnsley Gardens. There are two areas where Godfrey's ghost is usually encountered. First, eyewitnesses have seen a man in his late thirties or early forties standing near the main entrance to the mansion. When approached or after a few seconds, the apparition disappears. The apparition is sometimes preceded by the sound of hammering or sawing, so it is believed that the apparition is definitely of Godfrey continuing to work on his mansion. Barnsley's ghost has also been seen inside the botanical garden where he was visited by his wife's spirit in 1848.

The ghost of Confederate Colonel R.G. Earle has also been seen in Barnsley Gardens. Most often, Colonel Earle's apparition has been seen in both the botanical garden area where he died and near the family graveyard where he was buried.

BONAVENTURE CEMETERY
Thunderbolt

Although Bonaventure Cemetery may seem to be out of place in a book on haunted plantations, the most famous cemetery in Savannah, Georgia, actually started out as Bonaventure Plantation in the mid-eighteenth century.

In 1760 or 1761, John Mullryne was well on his way to owning several thousand acres in this part of Georgia. He transformed a 600-acre tract of land near Savannah into his primary residence and named it Bonaventure Plantation, which translates from French to "good fortune." In 1762, Mullryne built a massive plantation house for his family on the property.

Apparently 1771 was a very eventful year for John Mullryne. Before the end of the year, he and his son-in-law, Josiah Tattnall, had acquired approximately 10,000 acres of land throughout Georgia. According to some accounts, it was also the year that the plantation house built at Bonaventure was totally destroyed by a fire. As soon as the rubble from the fire was removed, Mullryne began construction on a larger, more impressive brick mansion.

The Revolutionary War was particularly devastating for Savannah and its residents. In 1778, the British Army took control of the city. On June 9, 1779, American and French troops attempted to free Savannah from British control. The second deadliest battle of the entire American Revolution has become known as the Siege of Savannah. The battle led to 244 deaths and approximately 600 injuries among the French and American troops, while the British only had 40 soldiers killed and approximately 63 wounded. In the aftermath of the siege, several of the French troops, led by Charles Henri d'Estaing, used Bonaventure Plantation as a makeshift hospital for the wounded soldiers. Many of the French soldiers who died at Bonaventure Plantation were believed to be buried in unmarked graves near the plantation house.

The war was also devastating for Mullryne and Tattnall, who were vocal about their support for Great Britain while all those surrounding them were loyalists determined to start a new country. Because of their loyalty to the British crown, the two men were forced to leave Georgia and told not to return under fear of death. In 1782, the 10,000 acres that both men owned were auctioned off to men who were citizens that would uphold the right for independence. The man who purchased Bonaventure Plantation was a patriot by the name of John Habersham.

After the Revolutionary War ended in 1783, John Mullryne's grandson, Josiah Tattnall Jr., returned to Savannah, Georgia, and purchased Bonaventure from Habersham in 1788. When Josiah Tattnall Jr. died in 1804, he was one of the first people to be buried in the family graveyard on the plantation.

The property remained in the Tattnall family until Josiah Tattnall III sold the entire plantation to Peter Wiltburger on March 10, 1846.

The following year, Wiltburger transformed seventy acres of the property into a public cemetery for Savannah residents, which he named Evergreen Cemetery.

Sixty years later, the city of Savannah purchased Evergreen Cemetery and city officials agreed to rename it Bonaventure Cemetery in recognition of the plantation that once stood on the site.

Today, Bonaventure Cemetery is a popular tourist attraction and is still used as a public cemetery. It has been featured in two separate books: John Muir's *A Thousand Mile Walk* (1867) and Jack Leigh's *Midnight in the Garden of Good and Evil* (1997).

In addition to being of great historical significance to Savannah, Bonaventure Cemetery has been featured in many of the city's ghost tours. According to the tours and local legends, the cemetery is believed to be one of Savannah's most haunted locations.

When people visit the Bonaventure Cemetery, there is no sign of the plantation house. The fact that it is not standing any longer goes back to around 1803 when Josiah Tattnall and his wife were hosting a Christmas party for some of the elite in and around the Savannah area. At some point during the evening, the house caught fire, which spread quickly throughout the entire mansion.

Realizing that the house could not be saved, Josiah ordered his servants to enter the burning mansion and carry the tables, chairs, food, wine, and other items onto the front lawn. There, the servants set the tables for Josiah's guests, who continued to party and drink for hours as the plantation house burned to the ground.

As the house finally collapsed, Josiah made a toast to his guests and threw his wine glass against the nearest tree. His guests raised their glasses in a toast and shattered them on the ground or against trees. According to some accounts, if a person walks into the older section of the Bonaventure Cemetery near where the old plantation house stood, he or she can hear the sound of people enjoying themselves, sometimes accompanied by the sound of breaking glass.

The most famous ghost believed to haunt Bonaventure Cemetery is that of a young girl named Gracie Watson, who was the daughter of hotel manager W.J. Watson. She caught pneumonia and died on Good Friday, April 21, 1889, when she was only six years old. Gracie's father arranged for her burial in the Bonaventure Cemetery and had asked sculptor John Walz to make a statue in Gracie's likeness for her grave marker. Once the statue was completed, Gracie's parents left Savannah, Georgia, and returned to New England, where they died several years later.

In the years following Gracie's death, visitors to the cemetery have claimed to have heard a young girl laughing and crying near the girl's tombstone. It has become somewhat of a Savannah tradition for people visiting Bonaventure Cemetery to bring a small stuffed animal, doll, or other inexpensive toy to leave at Gracie's grave.

Although not necessarily associated with the cemetery, there have been several reports that a girl fitting Gracie's description has been seen in front of the Pulaski Hotel, which is the hotel that her father managed at the time of her death. There are even claims that sometimes a small item owned by guests of the Pulaski Hotel can be found lying in front of Gracie's statue.

Bulloch Hall

Roswell

James Stephens Bulloch was a veteran of the War of 1812, in which he attained the rank of major. At the end of the war and throughout the 1820s, Major Bulloch pursued a variety of vocations, including politician, lawyer, and plantation owner.

Partially because of the name that he made for himself in the political arena, in 1838 Major Bulloch was offered a huge tract of land by entrepreneur Roswell King in exchange for his help in establishing a new township. Bulloch took King up on the proposition. This agreement and Bulloch's determination were pivotal in the formation of the town that is now known as Roswell, Georgia.

Immediately after acquiring the land in 1838, Major Bulloch constructed a large Greek Revival mansion for his family. As soon as the mansion was completed in 1840, Major Bulloch focused on expanding on his new plantation, which he named after himself. According to records, the primary crop for the 600-acre Bulloch Plantation was cotton, which was regularly tended to by thirty-one field slaves. In addition to the field hands, Major Bulloch had a number of house servants who helped with cooking, cleaning, and other miscellaneous domestic chores.

After Major Bulloch died in 1849, Bulloch Hall was sold by his widow to a family friend who allowed her and her children to live on the property. Five years later, his daughter, Martha Bulloch, repurchased the property, which brought it back into the Bulloch family.

Bulloch Hall was significant during the Civil War. In 1864, Roswell, Georgia, was overtaken by Union forces. General Sherman ordered General Kenner Garrard to bring in approximately 27,000 soldiers, burn down any mills in the town, and commandeer any local plantation houses to be used as either field hospitals or headquarters. Bulloch Hall was believed to be occupied by an unknown number of Union officers who maintained contact with Sherman to ensure that his orders were followed.

Bulloch Hall had a very significant history associated with at least two United States presidents. Martha Bulloch had spent most of her childhood at Bulloch Hall. As an adult, she married Theodore Roosevelt Sr. at the plantation on December 22, 1853. Together, the couple would have several children, including Theodore Roosevelt, who became the twenty-sixth president of the United States in 1901. A second child that Martha Bulloch and Theodore Roosevelt Sr. raised was a son by the name of Elliot Roosevelt. Elliot had a daughter named Eleanor Roosevelt, who married her cousin, Franklin D. Roosevelt, the thirty-second president of the United States.

With such a significant history, it is hard to imagine that from the 1950s until the 1970s, the mansion was abandoned and was in danger of being lost. In the 1970s, the city of Roswell, Georgia, purchased the property and restored the mansion to its original condition.

Today, the renovated Bulloch Hall is a historical museum that features permanent and temporary exhibits designed to preserve the history of antebellum Georgia. Bulloch Hall also offers tours for a much younger audience to allow them an opportunity to gain an appreciation of pre-Civil War life and culture.

Although paranormal activity has been experienced by visitors to Bulloch Hall for years, one ghost in particular has become synonymous with the plantation house. This ghost story has been the subject of many newspaper and magazine articles and has caught the attention of visitors and paranormal investigators throughout the nation.

According to local legend, a female house servant about thirteen or fourteen years old fell into a well behind the plantation house and drowned. It is not certain what led to the girl's drowning, but most believe that she was simply drawing water from the well and fell in. Others believe that the girl was actually murdered and thrown into the well to make it look like an accident. In either case, the girl is believed to have haunted Bulloch Hall for well over a century.

While the mansion was abandoned, and even after it was renovated into a historical museum, dozens of people have heard the faint cry of a young female pleading for help or weeping from the well. Although the well has periodically been examined, the source of the crying has never been found.

Another manifestation of the girl's ghost takes place inside the plantation house itself. As a house servant, one of the girl's major responsibilities was to light and extinguish the oil lamps and candles located throughout the mansion. After the girl's death, visitors to Bulloch Hall have had difficulty keeping candles and lamps lit for any period of time. At other times, candles and lamps are found lit throughout the house.

There have even been reports where eyewitnesses have seen the candles extinguish or light themselves without anybody standing near them. Even during the nearly two decades that the mansion was vacant, passersby sometimes saw lights inside the mansion that appeared to be either candlelight or lamplight. Although it could have simply been trespassers, it is thought that it was the ghost of the servant girl making her rounds.

While being renovated in the 1970s, Bulloch Hall was wired with electricity, and candles and oil lamps were no longer necessary. Although candles and oil lamps are no longer used, the electric lights and electric lamps throughout the house have been known to turn on and off on occasion at all hours of the day or night. Many believe that the electrical disturbances are caused by the girl's ghost carrying on with her duties.

EARLY HILL PLANTATION
Greensboro

In the late 1700s, Greensboro mayor and planter John Brown purchased several hundred acres outside of town and named his new plantation Early Hill. Less than a year after Brown and his family moved into the Early Hill Plantation House, he lost his youngest daughter in a horrible and unexpected accident. One summer day his daughter was swinging from a tree branch in front of the mansion. The weight and momentum of the swinging caused the branch and swing to collapse. She plummeted to the ground and was crushed to death by the large branch that fell on her. The unexpected death devastated Mayor Brown and his entire family, who never quite got past the tragedy.

Early Hill Plantation was not really involved in the Civil War and went through several owners from the late nineteenth to mid-twentieth centuries. A few decades ago, Early Hill Plantation was renovated and converted into a bed-and-breakfast that could also be reserved for weddings, parties, and other gatherings. However, the bed-and-breakfast has since closed.

Several ghosts are thought to haunt the Early Hill Plantation House. Most of the ghosts are of friends and family of Mayor John Brown.

Brown's seven-year-old daughter, who died when the tree branch crushed her, is the most commonly encountered ghost at Early Hill. Since her death, an apparition of the little girl has been seen near where Mayor Brown's daughter was killed. Unlike some hauntings that appear at approximately the same time that a person's death occurred, the apparition of Mayor Brown's daughter has been known to appear at all hours of the day and night.

John Brown's wife has been seen in the master bedroom that they shared. Rather than as a full-body apparition, only her upper torso is seen as a reflection in a large antique mirror. The ghost of Brown's wife is described as a very attractive young woman brushing her hair and is completely oblivious to any eyewitnesses. Like most apparitions, she is only seen for a few seconds before disappearing. It is also interesting that she is only seen as a reflection in one particular mirror and nowhere else in the bedroom or the mansion.

An unidentified older woman has frequently been seen in a rocking chair on the front porch of the plantation house. She is described as a woman about sixty or seventy years old with her hair in a bun, and wearing a long light-colored dress. Research into Early Hill's history has failed to positively identify the old woman as a resident, so it is likely that she was a family friend who visited the Browns at some point.

Although there are conflicting stories about the last ghost at Early Hill, there have been reports of sounds coming from the basement of the mansion. If these accounts are indeed accurate, it is believed that the sounds are of the chains of slaves that resided on the property when Brown owned it. According to legend, Mayor Brown was believed to have buried more than one slave in the mansion's basement.

EZEKIEL HARRIS HOUSE/ AUGUSTA MUSEUM OF HISTORY

Augusta

In the late 1700s, many tobacco planters from Virginia and adjacent states grew so much tobacco without rotating the crops that it made the soil infertile. As a result, several of these planters decided to just leave their tobacco plantations and establish new ones in southern states such as South Carolina and Georgia. Sometimes these plantation owners simply gave their new plantation the same name as the one they left. Having two plantations of the same name owned by one individual can be very confusing when it comes to doing historical research.

In the 1790s, Ezekiel Harris saw that several northern planters were moving to the southern states to establish new plantations. He moved to Augusta, Georgia, from Edgefield, South Carolina, in order to establish a tobacco inspection center. He thought that he could make a great living by opening one of the first tobacco inspection stations in the state. Before tobacco planters could sell tobacco in large quantities, the tobacco would sometimes go through an inspection station prior to leaving the state. When he realized that there were approximately twenty other such inspection centers, Harris decided to take a different route to make a living.

In 1797, Harris purchased several hundred acres of prime farmland and founded a new tobacco plantation of his own. During that summer, he built a beautiful Federal-style plantation house and in September of the same year built a very large warehouse in which to dry tobacco. Unlike most other plantation owners, Harris had no intention of being a planter himself, but rather had prepared the property to be sold to one of the planters who wanted to establish a plantation near Augusta, Georgia. Rather than purchase hundreds or thousands of acres of undeveloped land, Harris could sell a ready-made plantation to a planter for the right price.

Being a man of vision, Harris also noticed that when several tobacco plantations were established in an area, a town would often be started to accommodate the needs of the planters. Harris wanted to be involved with the designing and founding of a town that he hoped would rival nearby Augusta, Georgia.

Ezekiel Harris did not sell the property, but lived on the plantation for nearly ten years with his wife, Eleanor, and their children. Eleanor Harris died in March of 1806 of cancer, and Ezekiel decided to leave Augusta, Georgia, the following year and moved to Wilkes County, Georgia, where he died in 1829.

Although he did not sell his plantation, he did reach his goal by helping to found Harrisburg, Georgia, which is now part of Augusta's historical district. Today, the Ezekiel Harris House is operated by the Augusta Museum of History and offers tours of the house for a small fee.

Most paranormal enthusiasts who have studied the plantation's history claim that there are three distinct ghosts connected to the Ezekiel Harris House.

The oldest ghost associated with the Ezekiel Harris House is that of a soldier from the Revolutionary War. It should be noted that the Revolutionary War ended in 1783, over a decade before Harris built his house in 1797. It is likely that the Revolutionary War soldier's ghost has been around for considerably longer than the Ezekiel Harris House. Augusta, Georgia, was founded in 1735 and did play a major role in the American Revolution, including the Siege of Augusta, which took place in May 1781.

According to legend, the soldier either hanged himself or was hanged near the spot where the Ezekiel Harris House now stands. For nearly 200 years, the apparition of a man hanging on the porch or standing inside the main entrance of the house has been seen.

Not only have there been sightings of the soldier for over two hundred and fifty years, but another ghost is believed to have haunted the Ezekiel Harris House since 1806. The apparition of a woman has been seen standing on the porch and near a window on the second floor the house. It is believed that this ghost is of Ezekiel Harris's wife, Eleanor.

A third ghost that is sometimes seen on the first floor of the Ezekiel Harris House is that of an African American woman in her late twenties or early thirties. Her identity is not known, but she is believed to be a house servant of Ezekiel Harris or a person who lived in the house after Ezekiel left the property in 1807.

GAITHER PLANTATION
Covington

About twenty years after Covington, Georgia, was established in 1822, Dr. Henry Gaither purchased over 1,000 acres of prime farmland to start a cotton plantation in Newton and Jasper Counties, Georgia. While clearing the land to plant cotton, Dr. Gaither built a small two-story farmhouse for his family to live in while he managed Gaither Plantation, which he named after himself. To accommodate the vast size of his plantation, Gaither had between 130 and 150 slaves on the property to harvest the cotton.

Not only was he a successful planter, but Dr. Gaither was also a prominent and well-respected physician in the area. Dr. Gaither was able to handle both professions fairly proficiently until his death. After his death, his son, William Gaither, took control of the plantation. He and his wife, Cecelia, continued to maintain the plantation well into the late 1800s.

On November 17, 1864, approximately 15,000 Union soldiers led by General William Sherman marched through Covington, Georgia, and the surrounding area. Sherman made an agreement with the mayor of Covington that his soldiers would not touch any items inside area houses, but that anything left outside would be fair game for his troops.

A small band of Confederate soldiers used this agreement to their advantage. Being a Southern sympathizer and realizing that the Confederate troops were vastly outnumbered, William Gaither allowed some of them to hide in his basement and attic until the Union troops had left the area without incident.

After the Civil War, the plantation stayed in the Gaither family until 1929, when William's wife lost the property to a local bank for less than $30 in unpaid taxes. After the bank acquired the plantation, it was sold a few times over the next several years until it was finally acquired by the Newton County Board of Commissioners in 1996.

Today, Gaither Plantation hosts a number of events for the Covington community, including an annual Fall Festival and Civil War re-enactment. The property can also be reserved for private engagements such as weddings and reunions. Gaither Plantation has been used in several movies, including *Madea's Family Reunion* (2006). In fact, the entire town of Covington, Georgia, has been used in several television shows such as *The Dukes of Hazzard* (1978) and *The Walking Dead* (2010), and movies such as *Remember the Titans* (1999) and Rob Zombie's *Halloween II* (2009).

Other than Gaither Plantation being a prime location for movies and television, it is also the site of several ghosts and hauntings. The main dining room on the first floor seems to be the place in the mansion that has the most unexplained phenomena. Poltergeist activity such as doors opening and closing inexplicably and lights turning on and off have been encountered and recorded in this room for decades. According to several paranormal investigators fortunate enough to investigate the mansion, there have even been instances where the water faucet in the main kitchen has turned on by itself.

Footsteps have been heard in two bedrooms on the second floor and in the main dining room. Faint music and unidentifiable scraping or dragging sounds have been heard in the attic.

Although there have been some accounts of paranormal activity in the Gaither Mansion, most of the hauntings tend to be centralized in the nearby Harris Springs Primitive Baptist Church, which was not originally built on the property. Rather, the church was moved to the plantation site from a nearby location in an attempt to preserve it.

According to legend, the church's pastor discovered that his wife was having an affair with a parishioner. The pastor confronted his wife and cornered her in the church where he shot and killed her. Realizing what he had done in a moment of blind rage, the pastor turned the gun on himself and committed suicide.

As a result of the murder-suicide of the pastor and his wife, some sensitives claim that there is a heaviness inside the church itself, which is now vacant. There have been EVP recordings of two people arguing, a gunshot, and screams from within the church. Although not as common, visitors standing inside the church have also heard the sound of a choir singing a church hymn.

LOCKERLY PLANTATION
Milledgeville

Richard Nichols was a wealthy merchant who purchased several hundred acres of property to start a plantation in 1839. Immediately after taking ownership of the property, Nichols named his new plantation Rose Hill. After living at Rose Hill for a decade, Nichols died there in 1849. Nichols had no heirs to pass the plantation to, and after his death, appraisers were called in to determine how much his personal property was worth in order to pay off his debts.

One of the appraisers was Daniel Tucker, who saw the potential for Rose Hill and purchased the property for himself. Within a month of Tucker purchasing Rose Hill, the house that Nichols built accidentally caught fire and was completely destroyed in the blaze. By 1851, Tucker started construction of a new mansion on the exact spot where the former house once stood.

Soon after rebuilding the mansion, Tucker sold the property and moved from the area. Rose Hill was sold several more times throughout the rest of the 1800s and was finally purchased by Reginald Hatcher in 1928. At this point, the name of the property was officially changed from Rose Hill to Lockerly Plantation.

Since 1965, Lockerly has been open to the public as a historic museum and an arboretum. It hosts a variety of events for the community and local school children. In addition, Lockerly has received regional and national attention for its involvement with the Boy Scouts and various nature-themed summer camps for children.

Lockerly has developed a reputation not only for bringing the community of Milledgeville together since the mid-1960s but also for being haunted. Lockerly was featured on a second-season episode of *Haunted History*.

There are reports of at least three separate apparitions seen inside the plantation house, including those of a young girl, a tall man in a trench coat, and an older man with a beard.

The ghost of a girl in her early teens wearing a white dress has been seen on the first floor for over forty years. When she makes an appearance, she is usually accompanied by a tall, thin man wearing a long dark trench coat.

It is not certain who the ghosts are, but by the appearance of their clothing, they are likely from the mid-1800s, right before or after the Civil War.

The apparitions were first noticed in the 1960s when the mansion was undergoing extensive electrical and plumbing renovations. In the 1960s, plumbers were the first to see the couple when they were working inside the mansion. A decade later, electricians independently reported seeing the exact same ghosts when they were working on the mansion. Since then, the girl's and the tall man's ghosts have been seen several times by visitors.

Perhaps the most well-known of the ghosts of Lockerly Plantation is that of an old man with a long, gray beard. Although he has been seen throughout the mansion, the old man has never been seen at the same time as the girl or her companion. Some believe that the old man was a former owner of the plantation, and there are rumors that there is a photograph of the old man standing in front of the mansion.

STATELY OAKS PLANTATION
Jonesboro

Between 1839 and 1840, planter Whitmill Allen constructed a moderately sized Greek Revival home on a 404-acre plantation he had purchased a few years before. In 1858, Allen sold The Oaks plantation to Robert McCord. Soon after selling the property, Allen and his family moved to Smith County, Texas, where he died several years later.

McCord lived on the property until the beginning of the Civil War, at which point he enlisted into the Confederate army. From August 31 to September 1, 1864, the Battle of Jonesboro took place near the plantation. After the battle, Union troops took control of the mansion and converted it into a makeshift field hospital to treat their wounded and dying. Those who were not injured or caring for their comrades took the opportunity to get a much-needed rest.

The Oaks Plantation stayed in the McCord family until it was sold in 1889 to Calvin Orr. Not long after purchasing the property, Orr changed the name of the plantation from The Oaks to Stately Oaks. Over the years, the Stately Oaks Plantation House has been referred to by a number of different names, including the Robert McCord House and the Orr House, each referencing the previous owners of the property.

When she was young, Margaret Mitchell lived on her grandparents' plantation located near Stately Oaks Plantation. She and her family regularly passed the property when they traveled to and from town. It is believed that when writing *Gone with the Wind*, Margaret Mitchell patterned Tara after Stately Oaks Plantation.

The original Stately Oaks Plantation House is no longer located on its original site, but was moved four miles south to the historical district of Jonesboro, Georgia. That's where it became part of a series of historical buildings currently owned and managed by Historical Jonesboro/Clayton County, Inc. In addition to Stately Oaks Mansion, several other buildings of historical significance, including a tenant house, general store, and schoolhouse, have been moved here from all over the state. Today, the site is open to the public.

The ghost of a young, well-dressed man has been seen by dozens of people who have visited the Stately Oaks Plantation House since it was opened to the public. The man has been seen throughout the entire mansion, although he is most often seen walking through or standing in one of two rooms on the first floor and in the hallway on the second floor.

The second floor of the Stately Oaks Plantation House seems to be where most of the paranormal activity occurs. In addition to the man's apparition, the sound of footsteps and unidentifiable whispers can be heard in the hallway and in one of the bedrooms. The apparition of a young girl in a dress has also been seen in the bedroom from which some of the whispers are believed to originate. She is sometimes seen looking out the window. However, unlike many of the other ghosts that are seen in the window, this girl has also been seen inside the room itself.

Finally, the ghost of a Confederate soldier has been seen inside the mansion on the first floor. It is believed that the soldier likely died during the Battle of Jonesboro. Whether he is connected to the plantation house itself or the property where the historical buildings are now located is not known.

— FOUR —

LOUISIANA

CHRETIEN POINT PLANTATION

Sunset

Born in 1781, Hypolite Chretien moved near present-day Lafayette, Louisiana, in the early 1800s, where his father established a 3,000-acre cotton plantation, which he named Chretien Point. Upon his father's death, Hypolite inherited the property and continued to successfully run Chretien Point for several years.

In 1818, Hypolite met and married Felicite Neda, who was a very beautiful woman of Spanish descent. While Hypolite was busy taking care of plantation business, he had nothing to fear in regards to Felicite taking care of herself as she was a very independent and straightforward woman who freely spoke her mind.

In 1835, Hypolite and Felicite began construction on a beautiful two-story brick mansion near Lafayette. Once the mansion was completed in early 1839, Hypolite and Felicite were able to move into the plantation house. Although Hypolite trusted and respected Felicite, he refused to allow her to make any financial decisions concerning the management of Chretien Point. Rumor had it that Hypolite was so secretive about his finances that he buried large amounts of money in different locations on the plantation known only to himself and a trusted servant.

While the mansion at Chretien Point was being constructed, Hypolite became involved with the smuggling trade. In exchange for allowing smugglers to make brief stops at Chretien Point, Hypolite received considerable discounts on anything they had to offer. One smuggler who frequently visited Chretien Plantation was Jean Lafayette, notable pirate and smuggler who visited several local plantations including the Magnolia and Woodland Plantations.

Hypolite is believed to have contracted yellow fever from a blanket he purchased from a smuggler. Ultimately, the yellow fever led to his death in September 1839, only a few months after the mansion was completed.

After his death, Felicite took over the duties of Chretien Point and worked hard to make it as successful as possible. She immediately put an end to the smugglers' visiting the plantation and was known to personally walk the grounds on a regular basis to ensure that everything was in order. Some believe that she was looking for Hypolite's buried fortune.

One night several weeks after Hypolite's death, Felicite awoke to a loud noise from inside the mansion. She snuck out of her bedroom and found a strange man walking up the main stairway to the second floor. When he confronted Felicite on the stairway, she took off a valuable necklace and handed it to him. As he reached for the necklace, Felicite shot him in the forehead with a pistol that she always hid on her person. It is uncertain what happened to the intruder's corpse, but there are rumors that Felicite hid the body under the stairway.

Chretien Point was not immune from the destruction that so many plantations suffered during the Civil War. On October 15, 1863, Union and Confederate troops fought the Battle of Buzzard's Prairie right in front of the mansion. During the battle, several bullets and mortar rounds hit the mansion. A Union cannonball hit and destroyed a section of one of the upper columns of the house. Today, visitors to Chretien Point can still see one of the original bullet holes on the front door of the mansion.

Several ghosts are believed to haunt Chretien Plantation, including Felicite, the man she killed, and several Union and Confederate soldiers who died at the Battle of Buzzard's Prairie.

For years, Felicite's ghost has been seen in front of and inside the house. Felicite's apparition is described as a dark-complected woman in her twenties or thirties wearing a long dress. Generally, she has been seen walking the perimeter of the grounds, possibly looking for Hypolite's money or searching for trespassers. Sometimes her apparition has been seen accompanied by her children on the second floor of the mansion near one of the bedrooms.

The man that Felicite killed on the staircase is also believed to haunt Chretien Point. Since his unexpected death, an apparition of the man has been seen starting to ascend the steps, but it disappears within a few seconds. Visitors to the mansion have accepted the intruder's ghost and have given him the nickname of Robert.

As there were several Union and Confederate casualties at the Battle of Buzzard's Prairie in October 1863, ghosts of soldiers from both the North and the South have been seen in the fields where the battle took place. The apparitions have appeared so real that many eyewitnesses believe the men are actually Civil War reenactors until they disappear in front of the eyewitnesses' eyes.

The sound of gunfire has been frequently heard and even recorded by visitors to Chretien Point Plantation. Early some mornings, the sound of a bugler playing reveille has occasionally been heard in the field near the plantation house.

DESTREHAN PLANTATION
Destrehan

In the late 1700s, Robert Antoine deLongy acquired several hundred acres of farmland about fourteen miles north of New Orleans. With the property, he started one of the most successful indigo plantations in the state. Shortly after establishing the plantation, deLongy hired

Charles Pacquet to design and oversee construction of a new plantation house and surrounding outbuildings.

Pacquet spent from 1787 to 1790 building the Greek Revival mansion, nineteen slave cabins, and several other buildings on the property. During this time, Robert deLongy's daughter, Marie deLongy, met and married Jean Noel Destrehan in 1786. Jean Destrehan's father was Jean Baptiste Destrehan, colonial treasurer to France, and his brother-in-law, Étienne de Boré, perfected the process of making granulated sugar from sugar cane.

Robert deLongy stayed at the mansion until his death in 1792. The plantation went up for public auction in December of that year. Jean Destrehan outbid all other bidders and purchased the plantation to ensure that it stayed in the family.

By the spring of 1793, Destrehan moved into the mansion, took over the plantation's operations, and changed the name of the property to Destrehan Plantation. Destrehan stopped growing indigo and began to focus on growing cane sugar, which made him a fortune since, for a while, he had exclusive rights to use his brother-in-law's sugar granulation process.

Not only was Jean Destrehan a very successful planter, but he was also one of the four men entrusted by Thomas Jefferson to organize and oversee the transition of property acquired in the Louisiana Purchase in 1803. With the Louisiana Purchase, the United States purchased over 800,000 square miles of property from France for approximately $15,000,000, which averaged out to less than fifty cents per acre.

While living at the mansion, Jean Destrehan and his wife, Celeste, had a total of fourteen children, including their son, Nicholas. At some point Nicholas lost part of his right arm in a sawmill accident. Nicholas wore a long cape to cover his injury and began to sign his name as *Destrehan, Manchot*, which is French for "armless."

Another child of Jean and Celeste was Marie Elenore Destrehan. She eventually married Stephen Henderson in 1826. Henderson was a Scotsman who was already a millionaire by the time he married Marie, a woman nearly twenty years his junior. Through the marriage, Henderson acquired Destrehan Plantation and owned it until his death in April 1838.

Upon Henderson's death, the family learned through his will that he wished to free all of his slaves, give away the property of Destrehan, and have a factory built on site to make quality clothing and shoes for local slaves. His family heavily contested the will, and after nearly a year the will was not honored and the plantation remained in the family.

After Henderson died, Judge Pierre Rost purchased the plantation from Henderson's family. Ironically, Judge Rost had married Marie Destrehan's sister, Louise Destrehan, in 1830, so that when he purchased the property after Henderson's death, the plantation remained in the Destrehan family until Rost's death in 1868. After the Civil War, Destrehan Plantation was referred to as the Rost Home Colony, and the property was used to help freed slaves establish new lives by offering education, medical care, and other related services. Over thirty years after Henderson's death, Judge Rost helped his dream become a reality.

In the early 1900s, the property was purchased by a gas and oil company for mineral rights and was used until the oil and gas were exhausted in 1958.

In 1972, the property was purchased and the mansion completely restored by the preservationist group River Road Historical Society. Today, Destrehan Plantation is open to the public and offers tours for individuals and groups. It also provides educational opportunities for schools and other organizations.

As is generally the case with hauntings, there was a resurgence of paranormal activity after the Destrehan Plantation House was renovated in 1972. The majority of the paranormal experiences at the Destrehan Plantation can be traced back to three people who were associated with the mansion since deLongy acquired the property in the late 1700s.

Nicholas Destrehan has been identified as one of the most active ghosts found on the property. The apparition of a man wearing a cape has been seen standing both inside and on the front porch of the plantation house. Again, it should be noted that after Nicholas lost part of his right arm in an accident, he always wore a long cape to cover his right arm when he was in public.

The second ghost believed to haunt Destrehan Plantation is that of Stephen Henderson, who owned the plantation after Destrehan's death. When his wife (Destrehan's daughter) died in 1830, Henderson reportedly never got over her death and became somewhat of a recluse until he died at the mansion in 1838. There have been several reports of the apparition of a man who fits the description of Henderson seen in one of the bedrooms on the second floor. In addition to the apparitions, the sound of people in conversation has also been heard in this room.

The final ghost associated with Destrehan Plantation is that of the infamous pirate Jean Lafayette, who was a known associate of Henderson and often did business with him and other planters throughout Louisiana. Interestingly enough, Lafitte's ghost has also been associated with two other plantations in the area. The ghost of the man believed to be Lafitte is seen outside the plantation walking and looking toward the ground as if he is searching for something that was lost or buried. Because of Lafitte's connection to Destrehan and the reported sightings of his ghost, the mansion was nearly destroyed by looters in the 1950s and 1960s.

THE HOUMAS/BURNSIDE PLANTATION
Darrow

In October 1774, Alexander Latil and Maurice Conway purchased several thousand acres of land that had been used by the Houmas Native American tribe for hundreds of years. Realizing the impact of their purchase, Latil named the plantation the Houmas in recognition of the former inhabitants of the land. The following year, Latil built a two-story brick French Colonial-style plantation house in the center of his share of the property, which became a thriving sugar cane plantation that was running by 1803.

Shortly after the Louisiana Purchase took place in 1803, the Houmas was sold to David Clark, who expanded the plantation size by several hundred more acres to grow more sugar cane. Clark owned the Houmas for approximately eight years before he sold it to General Wade Hampton in 1811. Owning several other large properties, Hampton increased the size of Houmas Plantation to over 68,000 acres, which made it the largest plantation in Louisiana at the time.

When General Hampton died in February 1835, he distributed his plantation and over $1.5 million among his three children. In 1840, his daughter Caroline and her husband, John Smith Preston, took over the Houmas Plantation. When Preston did so, he arranged to build a large Greek Revival plantation house directly in front of the original house that was constructed by Latil in 1775.

Preston sold his share of the 68,000-acre Houmas Plantation to John Burnside in 1857. John Burnside was a native of Belfast, Ireland, who had considerable financial investments in the United States. He was one of the richest men in the South with a net worth of over one million dollars by the time he purchased Houmas. On this plantation and other properties in his possession, it was estimated that Burnside had over 750 slaves, which was the largest number of slaves owned by any one person in Louisiana prior to the Civil War.

John Burnside was one of the few plantation owners in the South who was not greatly affected by the Civil War. Many plantation houses were destroyed or commandeered by Union and Confederate forces to serve as temporary field hospitals or field headquarters. Union General Benjamin Butler attempted to acquire Houmas for his field headquarters; however, when Butler ordered Burnside to leave the property, he explained to Butler that he was not an American citizen, but still an Irish citizen. As such, if General Butler forced Burnside to leave his property it would likely have caused an international incident, which would likely have led to European involvement against the Union. Considering the potential consequences of having a foreign country as an enemy, Butler retreated and found another plantation to use as his field headquarters.

John Burnside died in 1881, and having never married, passed Houmas to lifelong friend, Oliver Bierne. When Bierne died the following year, Houmas was willed to his son-in-law, William Miles, who had served as both mayor of Charleston, South Carolina, and as a member of the United States House of Representatives shortly before the South seceded from the North. After Miles's death in 1899, the property was distributed among his heirs, and eventually the plantation house was sold. From 1917 until 1930, a blight destroyed all of the sugar cane grown on the property. After the blight, the family decided not to re-plant any crops.

Around the time when the Houmas Plantation House was built in 1775, two rows of twelve oak trees were planted on either side of a roadway leading to the mansion. Visitors soon began to refer to this roadway as the Houmas House Oak Alley. In the 1850s, John Burnside first referred to the twenty-four oaks as the Gentlemen of Houmas House, a name that has survived to this day.

After the great flood of 1927 destroyed countless homes and thousands of acres of farmland, the United States government implemented a program to build several levees along the Mississippi River. A large amount of wood was necessary to build the levees and rather than bring wood in from outside the state, it was decided to use local trees for the project.

Soon after the project began, officials came to Houmas House to use the Gentlemen in their project. A caretaker named Mr. Jones pleaded with them to not use the Gentlemen due to their historical significance. His pleas were ignored and sixteen of the twenty-four oak trees were cut down and taken to the Mississippi River to be used on the construction of the levees.

While en route to their destination, a horrible accident killed six-teen river workers. Although an attempt was made, none of the work-ers' bodies were ever recovered. Word soon spread that one man died for each of the sixteen trees cut down at Houmas House.

Since the time the sixteen trees were cut down, the sound of sawing followed by the loud crash of falling trees has been heard near where the Gentlemen of Houmas were cut down. Also, there have been ac-counts of the loud sound of water splashing near where the sixteen trees were placed into the Mississippi River.

Another ghost associated with Houmas House is that of a little girl about ten years old. Although the house was built in 1840, there had been no reports of this ghost until the mansion underwent major ren-ovations in 2003. The first person to witness the little girl was an elec-trician who was working on the second floor when he saw her in the hallway near a set of stairs. When he started to talk to her, the appari-tion disappeared. Fearing ridicule, the electrician kept this to himself until he overheard another laborer tell a similar story. After sharing his own account, it was discovered that several of his coworkers had also seen the little girl.

All of the workers described the ghost as a young girl about ten years old with long brown hair and wearing a light-colored dress. She was always seen walking near the back stairway of the mansion or in the hallway at the top of the steps. After the renovations were com-pleted, the apparition of the little girl continued to be so common that she was given the name *La Petite Fille*, which translates from French to "the little girl." She is generally seen very late at night or very early in the morning.

There are two possibilities as to the identity of *La Petite Fille*. One is that it could be Colonel John Preston's daughter, who lived at the man-sion with his family in the 1840s. While living there, she became very deathly ill. Fearing for her life, Colonel Preston made preparations to send his daughter by carriage to Columbia, South Carolina, to see a physician that was a close family friend. Sadly, Preston's daughter died in the carriage just as it was leaving the gates of Houmas House. Her body was brought back to Houmas and buried in the family cemetery. Devastated from the loss of his daughter, Colonel Preston left Houmas and never lived at the mansion again.

The girl may also be another resident of Houmas House. In 1900, General William Porcher Miles, his wife, and their seven-year-old daughter lived in the plantation house. One day, Miles's daughter died unexpectedly and was buried in a graveyard near the plantation.

LeBeau Plantation
Arabi

The original owner of what would be known as LeBeau Plantation was Francois Gauthreaux, who acquired the property in 1721 as part of a land grant. A few years after establishing an indigo plantation, Gauthreaux sold the property to Pierre Rigaud de Vaudreuil, who expanded production on the plantation to include not only indigo, but also cypress trees. Vaudreuil in turn sold the plantation in 1749 to Antoine Bienvenu, who kept the property in his family for over fifty years.

In the 1820s, Benoit Treme purchased the property from Bienvenu and converted much of the property into a brickyard, which was a unique but profitable use of the plantation's acreage. Treme kept the plantation for about thirty years until he sold it to Franciose Barthelemy LeBeau in the spring of 1850.

Four years after LeBeau purchased the plantation, he built a sixteen-room Greek Revival mansion. Construction started in 1854 and the mansion was completed in 1857, just a few months after LeBeau's death. LeBeau's family continued to live on the property for nearly fifty years.

In 1905, representatives from the Friscoville Realty Company approached LeBeau's descendants and purchased the mansion and surrounding acreage. Once they obtained ownership, the realty company converted the mansion into the Friscoville Hotel.

Twenty-three years later, in 1928, the Friscoville Hotel was purchased by the Jai Alai Realty Company and the mansion was renamed the Cardone Hotel, which was a cover for an illegal casino that served alcohol during Prohibition between 1920 and 1933.

Gun turrets were built into some of the closets when the hotel was renovated, just in case it was raided by the authorities. Shortly after Prohibition was lifted in 1933, the Cardone Hotel closed and remained vacant for several years.

LeBeau Plantation was purchased in 1967 by Joseph Mereaux, who had intentions of renovating the mansion. However, that never occurred and the plantation house began to deteriorate considerably over the next few decades until the nearby Domino Sugar Company acquired the property in order to park semi trucks.

In the 1980s, there was an effort to make the LeBeau Plantation House a historical landmark, but all attempts were unsuccessful. In 2003, considerable progress was made in finding funding and volunteer work to completely renovate the mansion, but after Hurricane Katrina in 2005, all attempts were once again halted.

For years, locals believed that the LeBeau Plantation House was haunted by a number of ghosts, including the spirits of one of the original plantation owners and slaves who worked on the property. These stories encouraged local teenagers and thrill seekers to break into the mansion to find proof of ghosts or to see some of the mansion's interior, including the gun turrets.

Over the past century, there have been hundreds of reports from eyewitnesses about the LeBeau Plantation, including accounts of lights coming from a second-floor window and the mansion's cupola, although there was no electricity running to the mansion at the time. Most believed that the lights were from curious trespassers who visited the plantation house late at night looking for ghosts or other adventure. However, some believe that the lights date back to the time of the mansion's incarnation as the Friscoville or Cardone Hotel.

It appears that most of the paranormal activity associated with LeBeau has been auditory in nature, with three distinct sets of voices heard throughout the property. People who visited LeBeau Mansion heard the voices of men with French accents calling out to each other. Some of these voices were recorded as EVPs by paranormal investigators. The voices were always heard in the same area, about fifty yards from the mansion, and would cease when a person approached.

There was also the distinct sounds of people talking and singing in the area where the fields were once located. These voices did not have French accents and likely belonged to the slave workers.

Voices heard inside the house included the sounds of children laughing on the ground floor and a woman crying on the second floor near where the light from the cupola has been seen. It is possible that since the woman's voice and the lights were in the same general vicinity, they were connected.

The reputation that LeBeau Plantation had for being haunted eventually led to its needless destruction. In November 2013, a group of men allegedly under the influence of alcohol and/or drugs entered the mansion looking for ghosts. When they were unable to find any signs of paranormal activity, the mansion was burned to the ground. All that remains of the mansion are the foundation and chimneys.

LOYD HALL PLANTATION
Cheneyville

William Loyd was originally a member of the famous Lloyd's of London. However, because of a long-forgotten disagreement, William was asked to leave London and move to America. The patriarch of the Lloyd family made an agreement with William. He would be given enough of the Lloyd fortune to move to America and make a name for himself. However, William would have to change his last name to Loyd (spelled with one *l*) and never associate himself with the Lloyd family or to return to London, England, again.

William Loyd agreed to these terms and moved to America in the early 1800s. After he arrived, Loyd passed through North Carolina and Tennessee before finally settling near present-day Cheneyville, Louisiana. He purchased several hundred acres of land and founded Loyd Hall Plantation. William built a two-and-a-half-story Classic Revival plantation house in the center of the property between 1816 and 1820. After establishing the plantation, he kept his family history a secret to all who knew him.

During the Civil War, William Loyd conducted business with both the Confederate and Union armies. Not only did he sell goods and supplies to both sides, but he was also believed to have acquired information from one side and sold it to the other for quite a profit. Eventually, this was discovered and he was hanged on his own property by Union troops.

Since Loyd's death, the plantation has been sold several times, and the first accounts of paranormal activity were reported in the early 1900s. There are no fewer than three separate ghosts that are believed to haunt the Loyd Hall Plantation House and surrounding areas.

During the time when Union troops occupied this part of Louisiana, a teenage Union soldier deserted his regiment with the intent of making his way back home. After wandering through the countryside for a few days, he came upon Loyd Hall. Thinking that the house was abandoned like so many other plantation homes in the area, he broke in and made himself at home. He found a violin, and being a musician, began to play the instrument for hours on the second-floor balcony. Little did he know that the mansion was not abandoned, but that William Loyd and his family were away for a few days.

A day or so later, the Loyds returned to the mansion and the soldier hid in a room on the third floor with the intention of leaving the mansion at the first opportunity. William Loyd went to the third floor and happened upon the unarmed Union soldier holding the violin. Loyd did not give the soldier an opportunity to explain himself but shot him dead on the spot. Loyd dragged the soldier's corpse to the basement where it was buried. Since the soldier was buried, the sound of a violin playing has been heard late at night on the second-story balcony where he was likely to have played a day before his death.

Another ghost at Loyd Hall is that of Inez Loyd, niece of William Loyd. Shortly after moving to Loyd Hall, Inez met and fell in love with the son of a nearby plantation owner. After dating for several months, the man abruptly cut off the relationship without an explanation. Depressed, Inez spent hours inside the mansion playing the piano. Late one night, a few weeks after her beau abandoned her, Inez fell to her death from a third-story window. While some believe that her death was accidental, others speculate that she intentionally jumped from the window to her death.

Today, the sound of somebody playing and running their fingers along a piano can be heard throughout the mansion at all hours of the day and night. Also, people have felt colder temperatures and a slight breeze near the closed third-story window where Inez fell to her death. On occasion, the sound of a woman screaming can be heard by this window.

Sally Boston is the third ghost that is known to haunt the Loyd Plantation House. Boston was a slave who took on the role of nanny and cook for the Loyd family in the years prior to the Civil War. Sally was thought of as a member of the family and was dedicated to the Loyd children and was very proud of her cooking ability. It was common for house servants to wear white outfits to distinguish them from the slaves that worked in the fields. In recent years, an African American woman wearing a white dress has been seen in the kitchen area, often accompanied by the smell of food being cooked, even when there is no food being prepared.

MAGNOLIA PLANTATION

Harahan

Not to be confused with the Magnolia Plantation in South Carolina, a cotton plantation on this site was founded in the mid-1700s by Jean Baptiste LeCompte II, who acquired several thousand acres of property through Spanish and French land grants. Although Jean LeCompte established a cotton plantation on the property, he did not live on the plantation itself. When LeCompte originally owned the plantation, he did not initially call it Magnolia Plantation.

Magnolia Plantation was founded in 1830 by his son, Ambrose LeCompte, who arranged the construction of the plantation house after he married Julia Buard on June 2, 1827. Originally, Magnolia consisted of approximately 5,000 acres with about half of the property being heavily wooded. Ambrose had the wooded area cleared in order to expand the plantation's cotton production. Through profits made from the increased cotton output and the sale of the lumber, LeCompte increased the total size of Magnolia to approximately 7,800 acres. In addition to Magnolia Plantation, LeCompte purchased two other plantations in the area.

The Battle of Mansfield took place on April 8, 1864, near Magnolia Plantation. The original plantation house built by Ambrose LeCompte was burned by retreating Union troops as they passed through the property. The mansion was rebuilt in 1898 by Nathaniel Hertzog, who reconstructed it as closely as possible to the original mansion. He erected the new mansion on the same site as the original plantation house, even using the original pillars that survived the fire of 1864.

Today, there are two separate sections of Magnolia Plantation. In 1994, the property surrounding the Magnolia Plantation House was donated to the National Park Service, where it is managed as a historical park. The National Park Service was able to transport over fifteen buildings from other locations to the site, including a blacksmith shop, a plantation store, and a slave hospital. There are also several buildings from the original Magnolia Plantation, including eight slave quarters that housed a total of sixteen families. The plantation house is not on the park's property and is owned by descendants of Nathaniel and Sarah Hertzog.

An interesting fact about the slaves at Magnolia Plantation is that many of them secretly practiced Voodoo. Many of the slaves at Magnolia became skilled artisans and produced some of the best pieces of ironwork and woodwork in the entire state of Louisiana. Their specialty was metal crosses. Unbeknownst to the buyers of these crosses, the blacksmiths often put subtle Voodoo symbols into their designs.

The main plantation house is believed to be haunted by an overseer who gave his life to protect the mansion. According to legend, Union troops retreating from the Battle of Mansfield approached the mansion to burn it to the ground. The overseer, a man named Mr. Miller, stood on the porch and refused to allow the soldiers to do so. The man was shot and the mansion was burned. After he was buried, the ghost of Mr. Miller is believed to have returned to where the mansion was reconstructed. Since it was rebuilt, the sound of footsteps has been heard inside the house and near where Mr. Miller was murdered. On dozens of occasions, items have been known to disappear, and it is believed that the disappearing items can be attributed to Mr. Miller's ghost.

The second location at Magnolia Plantation believed to be haunted is where the original slave cabins are located. In one of the two-room cabins lived a woman known only as Aunt Agnes. Many slaves sought her out for help. It has been speculated that she acquired her reputation as a healer through her practice of Voodoo. It is believed that the ghost of Aunt Agnes is responsible for other paranormal experiences that are known to occur in this building. People who have been in the slave quarters have seen shadowy apparitions, have had problems with electronics, and have even heard whispers in the room.

The sound of metal striking metal has been heard in the general vicinity of the blacksmith shop. Unlike most hauntings, where the room gets colder during a ghostly encounter, the temperature in the blacksmith shop has been known to rise. This would make sense considering the workers in the blacksmith shop used fire to create the metalwork.

Magnolia Plantation has developed such a reputation for being haunted that it was featured on episode four of the second season of

Ghost Adventures. After spending the night in the slave cabin and investigating the plantation mansion, the paranormal investigators concluded that Magnolia was indeed haunted by several separate spirits.

MYRTLES PLANTATION
St. Francisville

The original name of the Myrtles Plantation was Laurel Grove Plantation when it was founded by former Pennsylvania attorney general David Bradford in 1796. Bradford was a crucial player in the Pennsylvania Whiskey Rebellion of 1794, which in essence was a protest by farmers against the federal government's decision to tax whiskey made with leftover grain from the farmers' harvest. Rather than using currency to buy goods, the farmers often traded whiskey for the goods and services they needed.

After being pardoned by President John Adams for his involvement in the Whiskey Rebellion, Bradford moved his wife and five children from Pennsylvania to Louisiana, where he started to teach law. Bradford died in 1808 and left Laurel Grove to his wife, Elizabeth. In 1818, Elizabeth's daughter, Sara Mathilda Bradford, married Clark Woodruff. After they were wed, Sara and Clark took over the management of the plantation from Elizabeth Bradford.

Five years later, the legend claims that Clark Woodruff was having an affair with a house servant named Chloe. The secret affair went on for several months, until Clark stopped paying attention to Chloe and started seeing another house servant. Fearful that she would be asked to leave the plantation house, Chloe began to eavesdrop on Woodruff's conversations. Soon, she was discovered and Woodruff had her ear cut off as punishment for eavesdropping. Since that time, Chloe wore a green turban to cover up the mutilation.

The legend continues that Chloe remained a house servant for some time after the incident. Several months later, a member of Woodruff's family was having a birthday and Chloe was asked to bake a cake. She did so, but first added several crushed oleander leaves to the batter.

Woodruff's wife and children ate the cake and died from oleander poisoning. Woodruff was unharmed because he had not eaten any of the cake prepared by Chloe. When the rest of Woodruff's slaves found out about the poisoning, they hanged Chloe from a tree and threw her body into a nearby river.

After Elizabeth Bradford died in 1831, Clark Woodruff moved to Covington, Louisiana. In 1834, Woodruff sold Laurel Grove Plantation to Ruffin Stirling and his wife, Mary. The couple made several modifications to the original plantation house and almost doubled the size of the house in the process. While the renovations were being made, Stirling changed the name of the plantation from Laurel Grove to Myrtles Plantation.

Once Ruffin Stirling died in 1854, Mary was given ownership of the Myrtles. Taking care of the plantation was a very complicated process and Mary hired local lawyer William Winter to be her personal attorney for legal matters concerning Myrtles Plantation. While acting as Myrtle Plantation's attorney, Winter met and married Mary's daughter, Sarah Stirling. As a wedding gift, Mary gave the rights of the Myrtles to William and Sarah Winter. Together, the couple lived at the Myrtles and raised five children on the plantation.

On January 26, 1871, William was entertaining guests when an unidentified man on horseback came to the front of the house and called for him to come on the porch. William was uncertain who the man was, but the man again called for William and said that he had some business to talk about. Curious, William excused himself and walked to the porch to speak with the stranger. Without saying another word, the stranger shot William at close range and rode off. Clutching his chest and unable to speak, William returned inside the house, collapsed to the floor, and died. Although it was suspected that the killer was a man named E.S. Webber, there was no proof to support this. As for why William was killed, it is possible that he was shot because of a financial dispute or simply because of his personal or political views on the Civil War, which had ended six years prior.

After Winter's death, Sarah stayed at the Myrtles and managed it while caring for her ailing mother. Sarah died in April 1878 when she was only forty-four years old. After Sarah's death, her siblings helped with the upkeep of the mansion and the care of Mary Stirling, who died in 1880. The plantation remained in the family until 1886, when it was sold to Oran Brooks. Over the next several decades, the property was sold and divided several times until it was purchased by Marjorie Munson in the 1950s. It was Munson who first openly shared that she believed that Myrtles Plantation was haunted by the ghost of William Winter.

In the early 1970s, James and Frances Myers purchased the plantation and transformed it into a very successful bed-and-breakfast. After opening the Myrtles to guests, the Myerses embraced the paranormal history of the plantation and have shared their experiences with the world.

Myrtles Plantation is perhaps one of the most well-known haunted plantations in Louisiana and very likely the entire country. Some sources claim that the Myrtles has as many as twelve separate ghosts, although most of the hauntings center around the ghosts of William Winter, Chloe, and a very unique antique mirror.

The most famous haunting associated with the Myrtles is that of the house servant Chloe. Since she was hanged by other slaves at the Myrtles, people have seen a young woman with a green turban in the kitchen, the room where the children had their birthday party, and near the tree where she was hanged.

There are two separate areas of the Myrtles that Winter is believed to haunt. The porch where he was shot and died is said to be haunted by the apparition of a man clutching his chest before disappearing. The second area Winter is believed to haunt is the bottom of the staircase leading to the second floor. Although it is likely that Winter died almost immediately after being shot, some believe that rather than dying on the porch, he staggered inside the house and collapsed at the bottom of the staircase.

Another interesting feature of the Myrtles Plantation is the large antique mirror on the first floor of the house that is believed to be haunted by those with a connection to the Myrtles. People have seen and photographed apparitions in the mirror and say that the apparition of either a person's face or handprint (or both) has materialized in the mirror before their eyes. It is believed that the faces of Chloe, her victims, and William Winter have been photographed. In addition, some believe that an unknown Union soldier has also been seen in the mirror's reflection.

The ghost stories and legends associated with the Myrtles Plantation have been the subject of several magazine articles, books, and television shows, including *Unsolved Mysteries* in 2002 and *Ghost Hunters* in 2005.

Today, paranormal enthusiasts have traveled to the Myrtles from all over the world in hopes of experiencing firsthand one or more of the ghosts believed to haunt the plantation house. In addition to being a bed-and-breakfast, the Myrtles offers tours of the plantation house. It can also be rented for weddings and other special events.

OAK ALLEY PLANTATION/BON SEJOUR
Vacherie

Oak Alley Plantation was founded by Valcour Aime as a sugar cane plantation in 1830. Aime originally named the plantation Bon Sejour, which translates from French into "Good Stay." Six years after acquiring Bon Sejour, Aime traded it for another plantation owned by his brother-in-law Jacques Roman in 1836.

When Jacques Roman acquired Bon Sejour, he changed the name of the plantation to Oak Alley and built a Greek Revival plantation house with twenty-eight Doric columns surrounding all four sides of the mansion. It is believed that the number of columns was intentional. One of Oak Alley's most notable features is the twenty-eight oaks that line an alleyway eighty feet wide and eight hundred feet long. It is thought that the trees were planted in the early 1700s by a French settler who lived on the property for a short time. The earliest known reference to the oak trees is from monks who traveled through the area in 1722.

Jacques Roman died of tuberculosis on April 11, 1848, when he was forty-eight years old. His wife, Marie Roman, took over the management of Oak Alley Plantation. However, Marie was not good at finances and almost caused the plantation to go bankrupt because of her excessive spending habits. In 1859, she asked her son Henry to take control of the property and the finances. Although he tried earnestly to make the plantation a financial success, he was unable to do so, partially because of the onset of the Civil War.

Shortly before Henry took over Oak Alley Plantation, Jacques's youngest daughter, Louise, was walking down the main staircase when her leg was impaled by a metal wire from a hoopskirt she was wearing. The wound developed gangrene and required her leg to be amputated in order to save her life. After her leg was amputated, Louise dedicated her life to the church and moved to the God at the Convent of the Discalced Carmelites in St. Louis, Missouri, where she became a nun. Several years later, Louise returned to New Orleans, where she lived for several years before her death in 1895.

Realizing that the plantation could not recover financially, Henry decided in 1866 to put Oak Alley Plantation up for auction to help cover expenses that had accrued over the last several years. Oak Alley Plantation was purchased by John Armstrong for only $32,500, a fraction of the plantation's estimated value.

Over the next several decades, Oak Alley went through several owners until it was purchased by Andrew and Josephine Stewart in 1925. The couple invested a great deal of money to completely renovate the plantation. It eventually became a tourist attraction and was renovated again in 1998 to become a beautiful bed-and-breakfast.

Since 1964, several movies have been filmed at Oak Alley Plantation including *Hush, Hush Sweet Charlotte* (1964), *The Night Rider* (1978), and *Primary Colors* (1998). A few of the television shows filmed at Oak

Alley Plantation include *Days of Our Lives, The Young and the Restless,* and *Ace of Cakes.* Because of its reputation for being haunted by owners and slaves who once lived at the plantation, a 2008 episode of *Ghost Hunters* was filmed at Oak Alley Plantation.

There are believed to be at least four distinct ghosts that haunt Oak Alley Plantation, including the ghosts of three owners and two slaves.

Since Jacques Roman's death in April 1848, his apparition has been seen in the sitting room on the first floor of Oak Alley Mansion. Based on a portrait of Jacques Roman, a man fitting his description has been seen looking out the window in this room on several occasions. This room is believed to have been used by Roman as an office where he conducted plantation business.

Another ghost believed to haunt Oak Alley Plantation is that of Jacques's widow, Marie Roman. After Jacques's death, Marie fell into a depression, which may offer an explanation as to why she was irresponsible with the plantation's finances. After her death in 1866, Marie's apparition has been seen throughout the mansion and in the cemetery where she and her husband are buried. Her face is covered with a long black veil, which is consistent with the veils that widows wore after their husbands died. There is little doubt that the ghost is that of Marie, who is still mourning the death of her husband, Jacques.

Josephine Roman, Jacques's daughter, loved to ride horses and did so at every opportunity. She would often be seen riding a horse along the perimeter of the plantation for hours on end. The ghost of a woman riding a large brown horse has been seen doing the exact same thing, so it is believed the apparition is Josephine.

The most active ghost at Oak Alley Plantation is that of Jacques's youngest daughter, Louise. Her apparition is described as a beautiful young woman wearing an eloquent formal dress walking down the main staircase. As she approaches the steps where she was injured, Louise's apparition always disappears.

SAN FRANCISCO PLANTATION

Garyville

In 1827, entrepreneur Elisée Rillieux purchased several tracts of land with the intention of selling them to wealthy men in Louisiana who wanted to start their own plantations. Realizing that he could purchase property for a fairly reasonable price, he founded a start-up sugar cane plantation and waited for the right investor to come along to buy the property. He invested only $50,000 into the entire acreage, which included not only land to grow sugar cane, but several acres of swampland.

In 1830, Rillieux met Edmond Bozonier Marmillion and told him about the small sugar cane plantation that he had for sale. After negotiating a price, Rillieux sold the property to Marmillion for $100,000. Marmillion was in financial straits and thought that investing in a sugar plantation would help him financially. Through the twenty-six years that Marmillion owned San Francisco Plantation, he continued to purchase surrounding property and almost doubled the original acreage. To help with the crops, Marmillion also purchased additional slaves. To save money, Marmillion decided that the sugar cane could be harvested by hand and decided not to buy equipment that would have increased his harvest, and therefore his income, considerably.

In 1842, Edmond's wife, Antoinette, died of tuberculosis and left him to raise his two sons, Vaslin and Charles, while attempting to manage the entire plantation. Sadly, of the eight children that Edmond and Antoinette had raised, six would acquire tuberculosis and die from the disease.

Realizing that his sons would one day inherit the plantation, Marmillion decided to build a grand plantation house for them. It took from 1854 to 1856 for professional builders to construct perhaps one of the most original and beautiful mansions in the entire state of Louisiana. The seventeen-room mansion was a completely unique construction that some visitors described as resembling a steamboat from certain angles.

Although he invested a great deal of money into the mansion, Marmillion died only months after moving into the house. Shortly after Edmond's death, his oldest son, Vaslin, took over management of the entire plantation. Vaslin did not want the responsibility of taking over a plantation but realized the importance of keeping the property in the family. He also realized that Edmond had left very little money to maintain the plantation, which forced Vaslin to spend most of his savings in order to keep the property afloat.

Vaslin knew that other planters often named their plantations, but he was uncertain as to what he should name his newly acquired property. When a friend asked him what he was going to name his plantation, Vaslin replied, "sans fruscins," which roughly translates to "penniless" or "without a penny in my pocket." Vaslin's name for the property stuck, and soon the plantation became known as St. Frusquin.

When Vaslin Marmillion died in 1871, his brother, Charles, took over the plantation for four years. In 1875, Vaslin's daughter, Louise, was given control of the property but had no interest in the place. In 1879, she sold the entire plantation to Achille D. Bougère for only $50,000. One of the first things that Bougère did after purchasing the property was change the name of the plantation to San Francisco.

The property was sold a few times through the late 1800s and early 1900s. In the early 1950s, San Francisco Plantation was opened to the public as a tourist attraction by the new owner, Clark Thompson. Twenty years later, Marathon Oil purchased the property and placed several large storage tanks near the plantation house. In order to preserve the plantation house, the San Francisco Plantation Foundation was founded and was able to restore the plantation house to its original condition. Today, San Francisco Plantation is open for tours and can be rented for weddings and other special occasions. A number of other buildings were transported to the plantation from other parts of the state, including an 1830s schoolhouse and an 1840s slave cabin.

The most active ghost at San Francisco Plantation is that of Charles Marmillion, who inherited the plantation from Vaslin upon his death in 1871. Charles's ghost is usually seen in three separate locations inside the mansion. He has been encountered in both the main dining room and library on the first floor. In both locations, Charles's apparition is described as a tall, broad-shouldered man with brown hair and a thick mustache. He is described as wearing a long coat, which was fashionable in the 1850s. Charles was known to smoke cigars on a regular basis, so it is no surprise that the strong scent of tobacco can be noticed in both rooms.

In front of the mansion, there have been sightings of two young girls in white dresses sitting down in the front yard. They appear to be about six or seven years old and are facing each other as if they were having a tea party or playing a game. It is believed that these two girls are the daughters of Vaslin Marmillion.

Some visitors to San Francisco Plantation have personally witnessed or have heard accounts of the apparition of a man on the top floor and roof of the plantation house. He is described as an older man and most likely had been a laborer at the plantation at one point.

SHADOWS-ON-THE-TECHE

New Iberia

In the early 1800s, William Weeks and his son David acquired thousands of acres of land by taking advantage of land offered as a result of the Louisiana Purchase of 1803. By 1820, the two men had acquired over 3,000 acres of land, including Grand Cote, an island now known as Weeks Island.

When David Weeks was thirty-two years old, he met and married Mary Conrad, a nineteen-year-old woman who was living with her family at nearby Rosedale Plantation. Early in their marriage, David and Mary Weeks lived at nearby Parc Perdu. While there, she gave birth to two of her eight children, Frances and William, who were born in 1822 and 1825 respectively.

As his family grew, David Weeks purchased over 150 acres near present-day New Iberia and in early 1831 built a mansion for his new family. He felt that a mansion close to town would not only be beneficial to his family, but would make it easier to manage his vast estate and oversee the 160 slaves necessary to keep his plantation running.

In 1833, David Weeks developed a severe health condition. He traveled by ship from New Iberia, Louisiana, to New Haven, Connecticut, to seek the best medical treatment available. Upon his return to Louisiana several weeks later, many of his symptoms had diminished and he was able to resume his daily business affairs.

In May 1834, Weeks's health deteriorated again. He arranged to make a second trip to New Haven, Connecticut, for another regimen of medical treatment that had been successful the previous year. David Weeks would never see Shadows-on-the-Teche again, as he died on August 25, 1834.

After David's death, Mary Weeks took over the management of Shadows-on-the-Teche and Grand Cote with the help of her brother, Alfred Conrad. She took care of the plantation and her family as best she could until she met and married local landowner and parish judge John Moore. Mary supported her new husband's many political successes, including being elected to Congress on two occasions. Moore's Congressional responsibilities forced him to leave Shadows-on-the-Teche; in 1843, Mary's son William took over daily workings on Grand Cote.

Mary died at Shadows-on-the-Teche in December 1863, just after Union forces had taken over the property and were using the mansion as the commanding officer's field headquarters. Shortly after the Civil War ended, John Moore returned to Shadows-on-the-Teche, where he died in 1867 and was buried next to his wife, Mary.

It is believed that the library, the staircase leading to the mansion's attic, and the master bedroom are the locations where most of the hauntings take place at Shadows-on-the-Teche.

One of the rooms on the first floor has had reports of ghostly activity that are primarily auditory in nature. Although no apparitions have been reported here, the sound of furniture being moved across the floor has been heard day and night. It is believed that this was the planning room used by Union officers while the mansion was occupied during the Civil War.

Union soldiers are also blamed for several unexplainable sounds in the hallway near the mansion's attic. Over the years, people have heard the sound of loud footsteps pacing back and forth, a disembodied cough, and the muffled sounds of people whispering in this hallway. It can only be assumed that the source of these sounds is the ghosts of Union soldiers who occupied the mansion at the time of Mary Weeks Moore's death.

The epicenter of the haunting at Shadows-on-the-Teche is believed to be the master bedroom, where Mary Weeks Moore died on December 29, 1863. In this bedroom there have been reports of a misty or vaporous apparition believed to be the ghost of Mary Weeks Moore. People who have visited the master bedroom have claimed to experience a sudden drop in temperature, especially if the topic of Union soldiers is brought up in conversation. Finally, faint music such as that produced by a music box has been heard in this room.

WOODLAND PLANTATION
West Pointe à la Hach

In the 1780s, Captain William Johnson, a riverboat pilot from Nova Scotia, went into business with George Bradish to transport goods along the Mississippi River. Together, they made a lucrative business and in 1793 purchased several hundred acres to start a plantation in this part of Louisiana. Together, Johnson and Bradish became very wealthy men from the crops grown on their plantation. Eventually, Johnson decided to expand his horizons and put his share of their plantation up for sale in 1830.

Captain Johnson took what he received from the sale of his property and purchased several hundred acres near present-day West Pointe à la Hach. Once he established the plantation, he named it Woodland Plantation. Although Johnson established Woodland, he and Bradish continued to have a very close relationship to the point that Johnson named his youngest son after his friend. The two-story plantation house was built in 1834, and Captain Johnson continued to make a living from raising sugar cane and transporting cargo.

Once Woodland was established, Captain Johnson became business partners with infamous pirate Jean Lafitte, and the two secretly smuggled illegal slaves into the country, using Woodland as a drop-off point. Johnson built four two-story slave cabins to house the illegal slaves until they were sold. Although Johnson remained in the smuggling business for thirty years, very few people suspected that he was involved with the illegal slave trade at all.

Woodland Plantation is believed to have been haunted by five separate ghosts since the late 1800s. Of the several hauntings known to take place at Woodland Plantation, only one has been positively identified. After Bradish Johnson died in 1892, people have witnessed his apparition in several rooms on the first floor of the original mansion. Johnson is described as being well groomed and immaculately dressed, often wearing formal striped dress pants, a coat, and sometimes a large silk hat. Johnson's ghost is also seen carrying a long gold-tipped cane that he was known to have used when he was alive.

The ghosts of two young women have been seen on either side of a young man between twenty-five and thirty years old. All three are dressed in well-made period clothing, indicative of high social status. It is uncertain who these people are, but it is possible that the women were simply companions of the man who was likely a visitor to the plantation. These apparitions are always seen on the first floor, sometimes accompanied by a breeze and a sudden decrease in temperature.

A fourth ghost believed to haunt the Woodlands is that of a young boy. It is not known who he is, but the boy is described as about ten years old with short brown hair, and he appears to be so real that eyewitnesses have often mistaken him for a living person. When approached, the boy either hides around a corner in another room or simply disappears.

Woodland Plantation had a number of slave quarters near the rear of the plantation house until Hurricane Betsy destroyed them in September 1965. After Hurricane Betsy, the debris from the slave quarters was cleared and attempts to restore the mansion began. In the late 1990s, a Gothic chapel dating back to 1883 was moved to where the slave cabins once stood. Today, the chapel is known as Spirits Hall and can be rented as a reception area or dining room. It is called Spirits Hall because there have been dozens of sightings of the ghosts of former slaves standing in the middle of the reception hall, where their cabins once stood.

— FIVE —

MISSISSIPPI

Anchuca Plantation
Vicksburg

The Anchuca Plantation House was a Federal-style mansion built in 1830 by J.W. Maudlin and sold to Richard Archer seven years later. Richard Archer had moved to Mississippi from Virginia in 1824 and married Mary Ann Barnes in 1833. Four years after they were married, Richard and Mary Ann purchased the plantation and moved into the mansion. It was Richard Archer who named the plantation Anchuca, which translates to "Happy Home" in the Choctaw language.

While living at Anchuca, Richard and Mary Ann had a total of five daughters and four sons. Although he loved all of his children dearly, Richard developed a special bond with one of his daughters, who was so much like him that she was given the nickname of Archie. As she grew up, Richard and Archie developed similar interests in literature, the sciences, politics, religion, and other diverse topics that Richard's other children simply had no interest in whatsoever.

One summer while visiting Port Gibson, Archie met and fell in love with Josh Melvin, the son of Anchuca Plantation's overseer. It was likely that Richard became suspicious of his daughter after he noticed that she was spending less time with him and making excuses to leave him. Richard Archer discovered the relationship between his daughter and

Josh after he followed her one day. When Richard approached him, Josh said that he would like to court Archie. Because of the difference in social status, Richard Archer would not hear of it and forbade Archie from associating with Josh Melvin again.

This infuriated Archie, and she refused to speak to her father. She soon fell into a deep depression and isolated herself from the rest of her family. This isolation was so intense that when anybody tried to speak with her, Archie simply walked away and ignored them. Rather than dine with her father or other family members, Archie ate all of her meals by the fireplace in the mansion's parlor. Richard Archer was never able to reestablish a relationship with her before he died a few years later.

Within the first year of the Civil War, most of the Archer family left Anchuca Plantation. In the spring of 1863, the few remaining people who stayed at the plantation were forced out of the mansion. Because of its proximity to the Confederate front line, the plantation house was used as a Confederate field hospital during the Siege of Vicksburg, which took place in the area from May 18 to July 4, 1863. The number of soldiers treated at Anchuca is not known, but it is likely that some of the soldiers who died in the field hospital were buried in a field near the mansion.

After the Civil War ended, Jefferson Davis's brother Joseph Emory Davis lived at the plantation with his granddaughter from 1868 until his death on September 18, 1870. The plantation house is now a two-story bed-and-breakfast that is open to the public.

There are three ghosts that are believed to haunt the Anchuca Plantation House. These include Archie, an unidentified slave, and a Confederate soldier who likely died at the mansion.

The ghost of Richard Archer's daughter has often been seen standing by the fireplace in the parlor. Archie is described as a young woman wearing a long black dress. As this story has been reported time and again at different plantations, it is possibly a legend that evolved from the story of Archie and Josh's forbidden romance. And it may not necessarily be Archie; the woman is described as wearing a black dress, which is synonymous with a widow in mourning.

A second haunting associated with Anchuca Plantation is that of a ghost of an unidentified slave in one of the slave cabins. Although there are no reported apparitions associated with this haunting, many visitors to the cabin have heard the sound of a man with a deep voice speaking or singing. Often the voice is accompanied by a strong sense of oppression and hopelessness that some believe emanates from the cabin itself.

Finally, the ghost of a Confederate soldier has been known to appear in one of the bedrooms of the mansion. He is usually described as standing near the doorway of the bedroom and seems to be oblivious to anybody who sees him. Those who are close enough to the apparition have stated that when they look at him, he does not appear to be in pain but rather to be somewhat confused about his surroundings.

BEAUVOIR

Biloxi

The antebellum house that was Jefferson Davis's final home was constructed by James Brown, a wealthy cotton planter who purchased a tract of 608 acres from John Henderson in 1848. Brown supervised the construction of the summer home from 1848 to 1852. In order to expedite the completion of his summer home, he brought slaves from one of his plantations in Madison, Mississippi, and erected a sawmill on site. In addition to the main house, Brown also built two small cottages, one on either side of the main house. He used one of the cottages as his personal office and the other as a schoolroom for his children when they stayed there. The original name of Brown's property was "Orange Grove" because of the orange trees that grew there.

James Brown died in 1866, and his widow sold the property seven years later in 1873 to Frank Johnson, who in turn sold it to Samuel and Sarah Dorsey three months later. Incidentally, Mrs. Dorsey is the woman who gave the property its current name of Beauvoir, which translates to "beautiful view" in French.

In 1875, Mrs. Dorsey's husband died and she inherited the property. The following year, Mrs. Dorsey heard that Confederate president Jefferson Davis was having financial difficulties after the Civil War.

Being a diehard Southern supporter and a childhood friend of his wife, Varina Howell Davis, Mrs. Dorsey immediately invited Jefferson Davis to move to Beauvoir. Davis accepted the offer and moved to a little cottage behind Beauvoir in 1877. After Davis established himself at Beauvoir, his wife came to live there, followed a bit later by his daughter, Winnie. Mrs. Dorsey sold Beauvoir to Jefferson Davis on February 19, 1879. She moved to New Orleans, where she died on July 4, 1879, and was returned to Natchez, Mississippi, to be buried.

While living at Beauvoir, Jefferson Davis wrote *The Rise and Fall of the Confederate Government*. Being an avid writer with her own published works, Mrs. Dorsey helped Davis for nearly two years. After her death, Davis finished the work with the help of his wife, Varina, and it was published in 1881.

When Davis died, Beauvoir was inherited by his daughter, Winnie. Upon her death on September 18, 1889, her mother inherited the property. Remembering the kindness that Mrs. Dorsey had shown Jefferson Davis and his family, in 1902 Varina Davis sold Beauvoir to the Sons of Confederate Veterans with two conditions. First, the property was to be used as a veterans' home for Confederate soldiers and their families. Second, the property was to be used as memorial to Jefferson Davis and the Confederate soldiers who fought so bravely for the South. From 1903 to 1957, Beauvoir was able to provide housing for more than 2,400 veterans.

Today, Beauvoir continues to be a memorial to Jefferson Davis. Behind and east of the house is the Jefferson Davis Home and Presidential Library. Not only is there a museum and a tour for visitors, but Beauvoir can be reserved for weddings and other events.

With such a historically significant figure as Jefferson Davis calling Beauvoir home for such a long time, it may be expected that the first and only president of the Confederate States of America would have reason to haunt this antebellum house. In truth, there has been no reported paranormal activity with Jefferson Davis appearing at Beauvoir. However, the same cannot be said about his daughter, Winnie Davis.

Winnie's ghost has reportedly been seen standing in a window of the bedroom she occupied when she lived at Beauvoir with her parents. Those people who have witnessed Winnie from outside the mansion claim to see a long-haired woman looking out the window onto the great lawn in front of the mansion. Those fortunate enough to be in the bedroom when she makes her appearance claim that her apparition is so lifelike that they often mistake her for a real person until she disappears right in front of them.

There have been images of what appears to be Varina's ghost captured in several photographs over the years. One of the most convincing and significant photographs was captured during a wedding when the bride and groom were standing in front of a window of the mansion. When the image was developed, the very clear apparition of two people can be seen standing in the window behind the newlyweds. No guests at the wedding fit the description of the people and it is not possible to be a reflection of the couple. The two people seen in the window are described as a man and a woman wearing outfits consistent with clothing worn in the mid-1800s. It is believed that the female apparition is that of Varina. Although not confirmed, it is believed that the male apparition may be of Jefferson Davis himself.

As is common with many haunted plantations in the South, there are also several ghost stories of unidentified Confederate soldiers seen at Beauvoir. In a nearby Confederate cemetery, soldiers have been seen standing silently in front of headstones, generally only for a short time before they disappear. There are an estimated three to five separate Confederate soldiers haunting this cemetery. It is unknown if these soldiers are there honoring their fallen comrades, looking for their own gravesites, or just completely oblivious to the fact that they are standing in a cemetery at all.

CEDAR GROVE
Vicksburg

John Klein built the mansion at Cedar Grove as a wedding gift for his new wife, Elizabeth Day. Construction commenced on the three-story mansion in 1840, but the project was so elaborate that it was not completed until 1852.

While the mansion was being constructed, Klein and his wife went on a honeymoon to Europe. Although it is not uncommon for newlyweds to travel to Europe for their honeymoon, John and Elizabeth Klein spent the better part of a *year* on their honeymoon. While on their year-long honeymoon, Elizabeth arranged to have furnishings, clothing, and other items shipped back to Cedar Grove and placed in storage until her return to the United States.

Once he had reurned to Cedar Grove from his trip abroad, John Klein spared no expense in making certain that he had the best furnishings around. In addition to having the furniture shipped from Europe, Klein commissioned master craftsman and New Orleans resident Prudent Mallard to build several pieces of handcrafted wood furniture. Unbeknownst to his servants and family, Klein asked Mallard to include a secret compartment in the furniture to place family papers, gold, and jewelry. Klein's foresight in including the secret compartment actually may have prevented his family from losing everything after Union troops invaded the area during the Civil War.

In May 1863, Union troops led by Major General William Sherman approached and razed Cedar Grove and dozens of other plantations. Eventually, this congregation of troops would participate in the Siege of Vicksburg, which helped to determine the outcome of the Civil War.

While the war destroyed everything around her, Elizabeth Klein found herself alone. Her husband, John, had felt it was his duty to join the Confederacy to protect his land and the Southern way of life. Many of the servants had abandoned Elizabeth during the chaos. Many of her children had been sent away from Cedar Grove in order to protect them from the terrible ravages of war. Elizabeth herself was very pregnant and only a few weeks from giving birth.

It just so happened that Elizabeth Klein was related to General Sherman. Realizing that her pregnancy and family connection could prove beneficial, Elizabeth was able to get word to General Sherman, who allowed her to pass unharmed into Northern territory so that she could have her baby in relative peace.

While occupying the plantation house, Sherman arranged for it to be used as a field hospital for wounded Union soldiers. Perhaps it was his relationship to Elizabeth Klien that prevented him from burning the plantation house after it had served its purposes to him and his troops.

With the mansion being used as both headquarters and a field hospital, it was surprising that the furniture at Cedar Grove was not looted or destroyed. During the entire Union occupation, Sherman, his officers, and the hundreds of wounded soldiers were unaware that there was a secret compartment that contained all of Klein's wealth hidden in the mansion.

After the Civil War, Klein returned to the mansion and used the jewelry in the secret compartment to begin repairs on the mansion and to pay taxes that were incurred upon the property. The plantation property remained in the Klein family until 1919.

Cedar Grove may very well be one of the most haunted plantations in Mississippi, as it appears to have no fewer than five separate ghosts associated with it.

Plantation owner John Klein often smoked a pipe in a parlor on the first floor of the mansion. Usually, he would smoke in the evening while reading, relaxing, or entertaining guests. Today, visitors to the mansion can sometimes smell the sweet aroma of pipe tobacco being smoked in this room.

John Klein's wife, Elizabeth, has been encountered at Cedar Grove. She is usually seen walking down the front stairs leading out of the mansion. She is always described as wearing a long dress, and those who have seen her have the impression that she is walking down the steps as if to greet one of their many visitors. When approached, the apparition of the young woman always disappears.

Another ghost associated with the outside staircase at Cedar Grove is that of John and Elizabeth's seventeen-year-old son, who died after returning from a hunting trip one evening. While walking up the back steps of the mansion, he tripped and the loaded rifle he was carrying discharged, killing him instantly. As far as this ghost's manifestation, a person can hear the loud sound of footsteps ascending the back staircase followed by a loud gunshot. Although not common, the sound is occasionally accompanied by the apparition of a teenage boy walking up the stairs with a rifle over his shoulder.

LENOIR PLANTATION HOUSE
Prairie

French immigrant William Lenoir moved to Prairie, Mississippi, from Europe in the late 1830s. Shortly after his arrival, Lenoir acquired several hundred acres of property with the intention of establishing a large cotton plantation.

In 1847, Lenoir built a large two-story Greek Revival plantation house to oversee the property's day-to-day production. Upon its completion, Lenoir spent a great deal of time and money making certain that he had the best materials and most productive slaves to ensure that his plantation was successful.

Approximately three years after establishing his plantation, Lenoir and a house servant named Sara had an affair. Shortly after Lenoir started to sleep with Sara, she became pregnant. When she was no longer able to hide her pregnancy, Sara approached Lenoir and informed him that the child was his. Lenoir denied responsibility and the two got into a loud and heated argument. In an act of rage, Lenoir shoved Sara down a staircase. Both Sara and her unborn child died from the fall. After Sara was buried, Lenoir went around his daily business as if nothing had ever happened and even went to the point of denying the existence of Sara. The way that Lenoir treated Sara infuriated the rest of the slaves, and they decided that he needed to be killed.

Late one night, several weeks after Sara's death, a house servant greased the hinges to one of the doors leading into the mansion. The servant left the door unlocked before retiring for the evening. Four or five field hands snuck into the mansion and up to Lenoir's room when he was sleeping. In one swift moment, they attacked Lenoir, beating him and eventually slitting his throat before leaving the mansion as quietly as they had entered.

Guests who have stayed in the room where Lenoir was murdered claim that the events of that night sometimes repeat themselves. More than one guest has stated that they were awakened in the middle of the night by a loud banging or thumping on the bedroom door. This sound is soon followed by an audible heavy breathing, a gasp, and a horrible gurgling sound. Sometimes the bed springs will suddenly move for a moment at this point. It is possible that this is an impression of Lenoir's murder. Other guests at Lenoir state they feel something gruesome happened in this room, even if they may not be aware of the room's macabre history.

An apparition closely associated with Lenoir is that of a young African American woman walking up the staircase, apparently carrying something in her arms. When she reaches the top step, she pauses for a second and disappears. Although Sara died before giving birth, it is believed that it is her ghost ascending the staircase with her baby to confront Lenoir before she is pushed to the bottom of the steps to her death.

LONGWOOD/NUTT'S FOLLY
Natchez

Although Longwood Mansion is technically not a plantation house, it was owned and lived in by Dr. Haller Nutt, a wealthy cotton planter in the area. Nutt grew up at Laural Hill Plantation, and after inheriting it as an adult, he purchased more property. Eventually, Dr. Nutt expanded his holdings to include a total of five plantations totaling approximately 43,000 acres in two states. In Mississippi, Nutt owned and managed Coverdale and Laural Hills Plantations, while also owning Araby, Winters Quarters, and Evergreen Plantations in Louisiana.

Because Dr. Nutt had property in the Natchez, Mississippi, area, he wanted to build a house that was unlike any other. Dr. Nutt spared no expense to ensure that his mansion was the most unique and beautiful plantation house in Mississippi. He hired renowned architect Samuel Sloan to oversee the entire construction of the project. He brought Sloan in from Philadelphia and approved Sloan's design of a six-story octagonal house with eight rooms on each floor. It was an ambitious project, but as Dr. Nutt had other obligations, he allowed Sloan free reign over the construction of Longwood Mansion.

Construction of the thirty-two room mansion began in 1859, with the intention that it would be completed in two to three years. However, when the Civil War began, Sloan abandoned Longwood Mansion and returned to Philadelphia with all of his workers in order to support the Union cause.

At the same time that he had entrusted Sloan to oversee the construction of the mansion, Dr. Nutt spent most of his remaining money on purchasing the finest imported furniture to fill all of the rooms in the mansion. None of the furniture arrived because the shipment was interrupted by the onset of the Civil War. Likely the furniture was stolen or destroyed by Union soldiers who occupied the area at that time.

Having spent virtually all of his fortune on the mansion and lavish furnishings, Nutt had no choice but to move into the first floor of the partially completed mansion because he could not afford to go any-where else. He had already paid Sloan for his services, and knew that he could not reimburse Sloan for the work not completed.

By the time Union forces reached Longwood, Nutt had lost his architect and his furnishings. All that he had left were his crops. Un-fortunately, the Union troops burned his crops to the ground, literally leaving Dr. Nutt penniless and with no resources whatsoever. Dis-couraged at losing everything to his name, Dr. Nutt fell into a deep depression and died of pneumonia in 1864.

Today, Longwood is a historic museum that is managed by the Pil-grimage Garden Club of Natchez, Mississippi. It is open to the public for tours and can be reserved for special events. Nutt's Folly has also appeared on several television shows, including HBO's *True Blood* and A&E's *Guide to Historic Homes of America*.

Not surprisingly, the ghost associated with Longwood Plantation is that of Dr. Haller Nutt himself. He is most frequently encountered standing in or walking through the garden area located near the man-sion. He has also been seen resting in a chair in one of the rooms on the first floor that he was known to have frequented.

Dr. Nutt's wife, Julia, is also believed to haunt Nutt's Folly. Where-as the good doctor is generally seen in the garden, Julia's ghost is found on the staircase leading to the unfinished second floor. Those who have seen Julia's ghost say that she wears a pink hoop skirt and appears to be in her late twenties or early thirties. The identity of the woman was only revealed after a relative of the Nutts who had wit-nessed the apparition saw a portrait of Julia Nutt. He was surprised to find that the woman in the portrait was indeed the woman he had seen on the staircase. There have also been reports that even when Julia does not make herself known as an apparition, the strong smell of perfume is sometimes noticed on the staircase near where her ghost has been seen.

MERREHOPE MANSION
Meriden

Landowner and early Meriden resident Richard McLemore purchased nearly 700 acres in the early 1800s to start a modest plantation, which provided a fairly comfortable life for him and his family. Although not originally given its current name by Richard McLemore, the plantation is now known as Merrehope, which is actually derived from the words "meriden," "restoration," and "hope."

When his daughter, Juria, announced her upcoming marriage to W.H. Jackson in 1858, McLemore gave the couple 160 acres of the plantation as a wedding gift. Immediately after acquiring the property, Juria and her husband built a modest three-room Greek Revival cottage on the property.

Five years later, in December 1863, the midst of the Civil War, the house was commandeered by Confederate General Leonidis Polk. Realizing the strategic advantage of Merrehope's location near Meriden and other towns, Polk moved in with his family and made the cottage his Confederate field headquarters. Three months later, General Polk and his troops were forced from Merrehope as Union General William Sherman brought 10,000 Union soldiers through Meriden, Mississippi.

In 1868, during the Reconstruction period, Merrehope was purchased by John Gary, who moved into the cottage with his daughter, Eugina. The two added several rooms onto the three-room cottage, and by doing so transformed the style from Greek Revival to Italianate. The house changed hands a few more times until it was bought in 1903 by Sam Floyd, who added four more rooms, five bathrooms, and several columns to the original structure, which gave the house its current neo-classical architectural style.

The most active ghost at Merrehope is that of John Gary's young daughter, Eugina, who died when she was fifteen years old in Livingston, Alabama. Eugina's apparition has been seen throughout many parts of the mansion. She has been encountered looking out the window in a room now known as the Museum Room, in the first-floor library and parlor, in the main kitchen area, and walking down the front steps near the main entrance of the mansion. The ghost has been positively identified as John Gary's daughter because there is a portrait of Eugina in the Museum Room that fits the description of the girl's apparition. In each of the areas that Eugina's ghost has been seen, the temperature is known to drop several degrees just prior to an appearance.

On more than one occasion, Eugina's ghost has been photographed by visitors to Merrehope Mansion. One particularly clear photograph of Eugina was taken in the parlor by a tourist taking pictures of Christmas decorations in the mansion. Although there was nothing apparent when the photograph was taken, after it was developed the image of a teenage girl looking at the camera was clearly visible.

In addition to Eugina haunting the mansion's ground floor, a second ghost has been encountered in a second-floor bedroom known today as the Periwinkle Room. This particular ghost is that of an unidentified Confederate soldier who was likely stationed near the mansion during the Civil War. Although an apparition of the Confederate soldier is occasionally encountered, visitors of the Periwinkle Room are more likely to hear whispers, loud bangs that may be gunshots, and other unexplained sounds. Over the years, there have been several EVPs recorded of these whispers and gunshots.

MONMOUTH

Natchez

A local postmaster named John Hankison purchased a large parcel of land and built a Federal-style plantation house in 1818. Only a few years after Hankison and his wife moved into the plantation house, they both contracted yellow fever and died. Without having any heirs, the Monmouth Mansion and adjoining property went up for public auction in 1825 and were purchased by local entrepreneur Calvin Smith. After making several renovations and repairs to the

Monmouth Plantation House, Smith sold the property to Jonathan Anthony Quitman.

Although not known at the time of the purchase, Quitman would have quite an influential career in store for him. In 1835, ten years after moving to Monmouth, Quitman became a pivotal player in the outcome of the Mexican-American War. The reputation that he acquired for his involvement in the Mexican-American War was enough to get Quitman elected as governor of Mississippi in 1835.

Two years prior to accepting the governorship, Quitman had invested a considerable amount of time and money to make several changes to the plantation house, which transformed it from a Federal-style plantation house to more of a Greek Revival design. While Quitman and his wife lived at Monmouth, they raised a total of three daughters on the plantation.

Quitman became ill and died the evening of July 17, 1858. Although it has not been proven, many believe that he was in fact poisoned by abolitionists who did not share his political views on slavery and several other issues. Nonetheless, it was reported that Quitman suffered greatly for days prior to his death.

After Quitman's death and his wife's death the following year, each of the three daughters lived on the plantation with their husbands, who helped to manage the plantation's upkeep in the years just prior to the outbreak of the Civil War.

When Union forces invaded Natchez, Mississippi, in 1862, the Merrehope Mansion was all but abandoned. The daughters and their husbands fled the mansion and most of the slaves escaped. Several of the slaves that escaped joined the Union army to help in the fight against the Confederates.

Union soldiers then occupied Monmouth Plantation. Most of the ornate and expensive furniture was destroyed and used for firewood by the soldiers who were stationed there. There was considerable damage to the mansion itself after the Civil War ended, and when Quitman's daughters returned to Monmouth, it was nearly uninhabitable.

As is generally the case, the haunting of the mansion by Governor Quitman did not start until new owners of Monmouth made renovations to the plantation house. Originally starting as the sound of creaking floorboards and pacing footsteps, the intensity of the phenomena increased until the full-body apparition of Governor Quitman started to be seen.

Generally, Quitman has been heard pacing the hallways on the second floor of the mansion. Also, the loud sound of a person stomping or knocking things over in the attic has been heard, although the source of these sounds cannot be found.

Guests in Room 30 have reported being awakened late at night by the ghost of Quitman standing over the bed. He is always described as an older man in a military uniform. Those who have encountered his apparition say that he is seen for only a few seconds before he disappears. As a result, several people have specifically requested Room 30 in the hopes of having their own ghostly encounter with Governor Quitman.

WAVERLY PLANTATION
West Point

Planter Colonel George Hampton Young began construction on the Waverly Plantation house in the late 1840s. Although it is believed that construction of the mansion started in 1847 or 1848, there is no way to accurately determine the exact year because no documentation referring to the exact start date has been found. Colonel Young's wife, Lucy, died before the mansion was completed. After her death, Colonel Young moved into the mansion with his children.

Wanting to make a statement, Colonel Young had acquired the services of renowned architect and builder Charles Pond to oversee the construction of his plantation house. Pond did not disappoint Colonel Young, because when the mansion was completed in 1852, it was one of the finest examples of Jeffersonian architecture in the entire state of

Mississippi. Pond added a large octagonal cupola on top of the mansion. Although the cupola was of a Greek Revival style, it complemented the rest of the mansion nicely.

The ghost of Colonel Young has been seen on horseback near the family cemetery close to the plantation house. He has also been seen walking through the graveyard and near the perimeter of the mansion. In addition to Colonel Young's ghost being seen in and near the graveyard, there have been at least two other unidentified ghosts of men walking among the gravestones as if they were searching for a particular headstone.

Since 1962, the ghost of a little girl about four or five years old has been witnessed by tour guides and visitors to the Waverly Plantation House. The little girl's apparition appears to be so real that those who have seen her believed that she was in fact the actual daughter of one of the visitors. The little girl's ghost is usually seen on the landing of the staircase between the second and third floor.

Although no one is certain who the girl really is, there are two good possibilities of her identity. Dr. William Burt was a close friend of Colonel Young, and he and his family were frequent visitors to Waverly Plantation. Two of Dr. Burt's young daughters died inside the plantation house. His nine-year-old daughter died after contracting diphtheria. A second daughter, about three or four years old, accidentally hanged herself from a railing on the staircase leading to the third floor. This daughter died in the vicinity where the apparition is seen. Sometimes, instead of the apparition manifesting, the sound of a young girl crying for her mother can be heard.

It has been said that one of the rooms in the mansion is haunted by the ghost of a Confederate soldier that can only be seen in the mirror. If a person looks into a particular mirror that was part of the original furnishings of the mansion, he or she can sometimes see the apparition of a tall, thin Confederate soldier standing behind them. When the person turns around, there is nobody standing there.

WINDSOR RUINS

Port Gibson

Shortly after turning twenty years old, plantation owner Smith Coffee Daniel II came into the possession of approximately 2,600 acres near Port Gibson in 1846. Three years later, Daniel married his cousin Catherine Freeland. Through the course of their marriage, the couple had seven children. Sadly, four of their children died before reaching adulthood.

In 1859, Daniel began construction on a vast antebellum mansion for his family. He spent approximately $200,000 on a twenty-five room Greek Revival mansion. Also, Daniel arranged to have other amenities added to the mansion, such as large water tanks on the upper floors so that there would be running water throughout the lower stories of the mansion. The finest furnishings were brought to Windsor Mansion from all over the world. In fact, the house was so large that it is considered the largest antebellum plantation ever in Mississippi.

Perhaps the most unique feature of Windsor Mansion is that Daniel arranged to have a large observatory platform constructed on the roof of the fourth floor. This observatory was designed so that Daniel could admire the view of his entire 2,600-acre plantation. With this vantage point, he could see for miles in all directions.

Despite its sheer enormity, the construction of the mansion was completed in 1861, only two years after the project was initiated. Unfortunately, Daniel would never have the opportunity to live at Windsor, as he died only weeks after moving into the house. Ownership of Windsor went to his wife, Catherine, who continued to manage the daily affairs until the onset of the Civil War.

The observatory at Windsor Mansion was very beneficial in the early days of the Civil War, when Confederates took control of the house and used the observation deck to monitor the movement of Union troops. Eventually, Union forces acquired Windsor and transformed the twenty-five-room mansion into a field hospital for Union troops injured in the nearby Battle of Port Gibson in early May 1863.

After the end of the Civil War, Catherine Daniel attempted to renovate the badly damaged mansion, but eventually decided to sell Windsor. The new owners continued to make repairs until it was in its original antebellum state. The mansion remained in great condition for several years and was known to host parties and other gatherings for the area's elite.

On February 17, 1890, a guest walked onto the third- or fourth-floor balcony to admire the view. The man had been smoking a cigar and put it out. However, the cigar was not extinguished and soon caught the balcony, and eventually the third floor, on fire. By the time the owners of the plantation returned to Windsor from their errands in town, the mansion was completely in flames. As the fire started on the third floor and was working its way down to the first, there was nothing that anyone could do but to watch the beautiful mansion burn to the ground.

The owners of Windsor decided not to rebuild; the fire left only twenty-three columns as a testament that the largest antebellum plantation house in Mississippi had once stood on the site. The property was abandoned for decades until it was designated a historical site by the National Register of Historic Places.

Most of the ghostly phenomena encountered at the Windsor Ruins are auditory, olfactory, or tactile rather than visual in nature. There have been several cases where people who visited Windsor claimed to have had the feeling of being pushed or otherwise touched by an unseen hand. Other times, there are visitors who have said they were hit with an unexpected gust of warm air, sometimes accompanied by the smell of burning wood. Any investigation to find the source of the smell is always unsuccessful.

People who visit Windsor Ruins will sometimes hear whispers of conversation and period music as if a party were being held. There have been several clear recordings of these sounds collected by ghost hunters and visitors to Windsor Ruins. One particular EVP may be that of the man who accidentally started the fire that destroyed the mansion in 1890. The EVP is of a man who is clearly heard saying, "It's all my fault."

As for apparitions, there is one recurrent apparition seen at the Ruins. It is of a Union soldier ascending a phantom set of steps where the main staircase to the mansion was located before the fire. The soldier appears to be oblivious to the fact that the staircase, let alone the entire mansion, is no longer standing.

── SIX ──

NORTH CAROLINA

BELLAMY MANSION/BELLAMY MANSION MUSEUM
Wilmington

Bellamy Mansion in Wilmington, North Carolina, was built by physician and plantation owner Dr. John Dillard Bellamy. The twenty-two room Greek Revival mansion was built between 1858 and 1861. Bellamy Mansion was not a plantation house, since it was located in Wilmington, North Carolina; rather, it was an urban base of operations from which Dr. Bellamy managed no fewer than three large plantations, which included Belvedere, Groveley, and Orton Plantations.

Bellamy Mansion was also used as a refuge when Dr. Bellamy and his family did not want to stay at one of his plantation houses. Because of its central location to all of his plantations, Bellamy used the mansion as his primary residence.

On March 1, 1865, less than four years after the construction of Bellamy Mansion, Union General Joseph R. Hawley forced Dr. Bellamy from the mansion and used it as field headquarters for several months. Due to the Civil War and a yellow fever outbreak, Bellamy and his family had to alternate living between his other rural plantation houses for four years until they were finally able to return to Bellamy Mansion.

Today, the Bellamy Mansion Museum is open to the public for guided and self-guided tours. Inside, visitors can see some of the original furnishings owned by Dr. Bellamy and his family. There is an art gallery that features several local and regional artists in a variety of exhibits. The mansion is used for a number of local functions and fundraisers. The Bellamy Mansion Museum can also be rented for special events.

According to various sources, several ghosts are believed to haunt Bellamy Mansion, including family members, Confederate and Union soldiers, and specters that have yet to be identified.

Soon after Dr. Bellamy's wife, Ellen, died at the mansion in 1946 at the age of ninety-four, people said that her ghost had been encountered in the second-floor bedroom in which she died and throughout the rest of the mansion. Ellen has been seen peering out her bedroom window, and it was confirmed that no staff or visitors were inside the mansion at the time of the sighting because the mansion was closed for the evening.

Another paranormal event that may be attributed to Ellen concerns her wheelchair, which is on display at the Bellamy Museum. Over the years, it has been said that on several occasions, her wheelchair has been found in locations throughout the mansion other than the area where it is on display. As with the apparition, the wheelchair's movement has always taken place late at night after the mansion is closed.

A third manifestation that can be attributed to Ellen Bellamy is located on the third floor, where an older couple in period clothing has been seen standing by a large, decorative window. The description of the old woman is consistent with the apparition of Ellen that is seen looking out of the second-floor bedroom window.

Children laughing and playing have been heard on the first floor of the mansion. On a few occasions, two or three children have been seen playing on the porch and in one room on the first floor. These ghosts are likely not any of Dr. Bellamy's ten children, as all except one infant lived well into adulthood.

There are two other hauntings connected with the mansion that are not believed to be attributed to the Bellamy family. During General Hawley's occupation of Bellamy Mansion, more than one Union soldier was known to have died on the site. There are reports of an apparition that appears for a few seconds of a Union soldier standing at attention near the house. It is possible that he was a guard stationed in front of the main entrance to the mansion.

The apparition of a second Union soldier is accompanied by a young woman standing outside the mansion near a window on the first floor. This particular soldier does not appear to be the same as the soldier stationed at the front entrance. Rather, it is likely a Union soldier having a secret rendezvous with a local young lady, which was not uncommon during the Civil War. Near this area, separate EVPs of male and female voices have been recorded, which are believed to be the Union soldier and his companion.

Finally, many people have seen the ghost of what has become known as the Man in Black. This apparition has been described as an older man with long dark hair and a long black beard. He is always seen wearing a well-tailored black business suit. This does not fit the description of Dr. Bellamy, and it is uncertain exactly who this man was when he was alive. He could have been a business associate of Dr. Bellamy or even a visitor to the mansion while it was occupied by General Hawley.

FOSCUE PLANTATION
Pollocksville

In the late 1700s Simon and Nancy Foscue purchased a 500-acre tract of land just north of present-day Pollacksville, North Carolina, and established Foscue Plantation. On September 22, 1801, Simon Foscue Sr. deeded the property to his son, Simon Foscue Jr. It is likely that the plantation was a wedding gift to Simon Jr., as he married Christina Rhem on April 30, 1801.

In 1824, Simon Foscue Jr. built a larger three-story brick plantation house near the site of the original two-story house that his father had built. As with the first house, Foscue Jr. arranged to have each brick for his mansion made by hand on the site of the plantation. This ensured that there was a fresh supply of bricks that were personally inspected for quality.

In addition to being a successful planter, Simon Foscue Jr. was appointed justice of the peace for Pollacksville, North Carolina, by Governor Hawkins in 1813, a position that he retained until shortly before his death in 1830.

Simon Foscue Jr. willed the property of 500 acres and twenty-five slaves to his son, John Edward Foscue, upon his death in 1830. John Foscue, in turn, willed Foscue Plantation to his wife, Caroline, when he died in 1849.

Foscue Plantaton continued to thrive as a plantation after Caroline took control. Records indicate that she increased the acreage of the plantation considerably. To manage the larger site of Foscue Plantation, she had also increased the number of slaves to forty-eight by the beginning of the Civil War. After the Civil War ended, the Foscues were fortunate enough to hold onto the property, unlike many other planation owners who lost everything. The Foscues have kept the property and mansion in the family to this day.

Today, Foscue Plantation has been carefully restored to its original condition to allow visitors to fully experience the property as it was during the nineteenth century. Foscue Plantation is open to the public and has guided and self-guided tours of the mansion and surrounding property. Foscue Plantation can also be reserved for special events such as weddings and reunions.

The ghosts of former slaves are believed to haunt the third floor and attic of the Foscue Plantation House. Visitors to the house have heard the sounds of cries and heavy chains rattling from the attic, even though the door leading to the attic is locked from the outside. Although unconfirmed, there were rumors that Foscue kept slaves in the attic on occasion.

GRIMESLAND PLANTATION
Grimesland

In the 1760s, Dempsie Grimes moved to North Carolina from Virginia, where he founded Avon Plantation shortly after his arrival. When he was barely out of his teens, Dempsie's son William purchased over a thousand acres a few miles downriver from Avon and started his own plantation that he named Grimesland.

Upon his death, William passed the plantation to his son, Brian Grimes, who continued the tradition of being a planter. Brian Grimes Jr. was born on the plantation on November 2, 1828, and in 1844, when he was only fifteen years old, he enrolled into the University of North Carolina. Being a gifted student, Bryan Grimes Jr. graduated college in 1848 at nineteen years of age. As a graduation gift, Bryan Grimes Jr. was given Grimesland Plantation with over one hundred slaves to tend the fields. He spent the next twelve years making Grimesland one of the most profitable and well-respected plantations in the state.

Bryan Grimes Jr. found himself becoming drawn into the political arena as the tensions between the North and the South escalated. In May 1861, Bryan Grimes Jr. was one of the signers of the ordinance that made North Carolina's secession from the United States a reality. Shortly thereafter, he enlisted into the Confederate army, where he was given the rank of major. During the Civil War, Grimes Jr. bravely fought at such battles as the Seven Days Battle, the Battle of Fredericksburg, the Battle of Fort Manassas, the Battle of Spotsylvania, and the Battle of Gettysburg. By the end of the Civil War, the seasoned veteran had achieved the high rank of brigadier general, one of the highest ranks ever awarded to an officer.

After the Civil War, Bryan Grimes Jr. and his wife, Charlotte, returned to Grimesland in 1867 to rebuild the plantation and raise a family of their own. While at Grimesland, Bryan Grimes Jr. and Charlotte raised a total of ten children. Bryan resumed where he left off prior to enlisting, and again Grimesland became very profitable. Grimes shared a large portion of the plantation's profits with his community and with the University of North Carolina on a regular basis.

On August 14, 1880, while riding back from attending a political convention in nearby Little Washington, North Carolina, Grimes's buggy was ambushed by an unknown assailant. The man pulled his gun on Grimes and shot him at close range, killing him instantly. A teenage boy who was riding with Grimes at the time of the attack was not harmed and returned the buggy with Grimes's body back to Grimesland Plantation. Although a man by the name of William Parker was arrested and tried for Grimes's murder, he was found not guilty of the charge. In honor of the bravery, dedication, and loyalty that Bryan Grimes Jr. showed in support of the southern cause, Little Washington, North Carolina, changed its name to Grimesland, North Carolina, in 1893.

After Grimes's death, the property was sold a handful of times in the early twentieth century and then became abandoned for several years. In 2004 or 2005, a private individual purchased Grimesland Plantation and painstakingly renovated the plantation house, the barn, and the slave quarters to their original condition. Although Bryan Grimes Jr. played a very significant part in the Civil War and in North Carolina's history, please keep in mind that Grimesland is privately owned. Out of respect for the owner's privacy, it is advisable not to approach the property without prior permission.

According to a number of sources, there are believed to be two separate hauntings that may be associated with Grimesland Plantation.

The ghost of a young girl has been seen and photographed hiding behind a tree near the main plantation house. She appears to be five years old and seems to have a fun-loving, carefree demeanor. The little girl has light brown hair and wears a light-colored dress. Although her identity is not known, she could be the ghost of Zilpha Ann Grimes, daughter of Bryan Grimes Sr., who died in 1822 at three years of age. More likely, the ghost is that of a daughter of a visitor to Grimesland.

Another ghost that has been seen at Grimesland is that of a woman looking out a window on the main floor of the plantation house. This woman has been seen by individuals for nearly a century. It is believed that this apparition is the ghost of Bryan Grimes Jr.'s wife, Charlotte, who died in 1920 in Grimesland, North Carolina.

HARMONY HALL PLANTATION
White Oak

Colonel James Richardson acquired a 12,000-acre plot of land near present-day White Oak, North Carolina, from King George II for his service in the French and Indian War. Although the actual date of this transfer of land is uncertain, there is documentation of Richardson's ownership of the property prior to 1768. Richardson had specifically requested this particular area because he and his brother were once shipwrecked near Cape Hattaras, North Carolina, and spent several months repairing their ship before they could return to their home in Stonington, Connecticut.

Once Richardson acquired the property, he immediately began construction of a two-story gabled plantation house, which remained in the Richardson family until his grandson Edmund Richardson sold the property in 1865 and moved to Texas.

Documentation of ownership was lost for several years, but property records dating to 1874 indicate that a man by the name of Layton purchased Harmony Hall. The plantation stayed in the Layton family until 1962, when the property was donated by N. Arthur Layton to the Bladen County, North Carolina Historical Society as a memorial to the Layton family and Colonel Richardson. Layton also wanted to ensure that the plantation's history would be preserved for generations to come.

Today, Harmony Hall has become a time capsule of sorts. In addition to the house, the property has a log cabin, chapel, two country stores, a corn crib, and several other period buildings that were transported from other parts of the state and restored as much as possible to their original condition.

In at least one of the buildings, the sound of two men in a heated discussion has been heard. The first reported occurrence of this took place in 1971 when a volunteer was cleaning a room late at night. Since then, there have been dozens of reports of the two men talking, as well as miscellaneous apparitions in various buildings on the campus. The apparitions include a young man in period clothing that is believed to be James Richardson.

MORDECAI PLANTATION
Raleigh

When Joel Lane moved to this area in the 1760s, long before Raleigh had been established, he purchased 5,000 acres of land to start a plantation for his new family. He was very crucial in the development of this part of North Carolina, including the development of Wake County in 1770. Once Wake County had been established, he sold 1,000 acres of his plantation to help found the city of Raleigh, North Carolina, in 1792.

Joel Lane realized that his oldest son, Henry, would one day inherit the plantation, so Joel built a large plantation house for Henry in 1785. Today, the Mordecai Plantation House is the oldest residence in Raleigh, North Carolina, still on its original foundation.

Not having a son, Henry Lane willed the plantation to his oldest daughter, Margaret. Margaret married Moses Mordecai Jr., and he took ownership of the property and renamed it Mordecai Plantation. One of the first things Moses did after taking over the plantation was to make additions to the original plantation house. In 1824, Mordecai hired state architect William Nichols to add four rooms, completely converting it into a Greek Revival mansion.

Moses Mordecai Jr. became a well-known lawyer in the Raleigh, North Carolina, area and was a member of the 1805 Court of Conference. After marrying Margaret, Moses focused less on his duties as a lawyer and more on his responsibilities as a planter. He also spent a considerable amount of time on his political career, and by doing so was eventually elected to the North Carolina State Legislature.

Moses and Margaret Mordecai had three children: Henry, Jacob, and Ellen. After Margaret died in 1824, Moses married her younger sister, Ann. Henry took control of Mordecai Plantation upon Moses's death. Following in his father's footsteps, Henry also became interested in politics and was elected to the North Carolina State Legislature.

Today, the Mordecai Square Historic Park is managed by the Parks, Recreation, and Cultural Resources Department of the City of Raleigh, North Carolina. In addition to the Mordecai House, there are three other historical buildings that have been brought to and reconstructed at the three-acre park. These include the Allen Kitchen, Badger Iredell Law Office, and St. Mark's Chapel.

Since before the property was opened to the public, there have been rumors of several ghosts that are connected with the Mordecai Plantation House. On Sy-Fy's *Ghost Hunters,* TAPS featured Mordecai Plantation in episode five of the second season of the series.

Other than the Mordecai House, the most significant building at the park is the house where seventeenth president Andrew Johnson was born in 1808. The small wood structure was originally described as an outbuilding or detached kitchen that had been converted into a small living quarters. The house was not originally built near the Mordecai Plantation, but through a succession of four moves, the one-story building was finally placed at Mordecai Park in 1975.

The most active haunting at the Mordecai House is that of Mary Willis Mordecai, daughter of Henry Mordecai. Mary married William Turk on January 12, 1881, at the Mordecai House, where they raised two children. Mary died in 1937 of a brain hemorrhage. After her death, people began to believe that she haunted the plantation house.

According to most accounts, Mary's apparition is seen in the drawing room wearing a light gray dress. The sound of a piano playing softly has been heard coming from the drawing room where Mary's apparition is seen. A few notes of piano music have been recorded as an EVP by various paranormal investigators, but not to the point where a melody or song can be identified.

SMITH-MCDOWELL HOUSE
Asheville

A several-hundred-acre piece of property was given to Colonel Daniel Smith for his service during the Revolutionary War. Soon after settling on the property, Colonel Smith's wife gave birth to their first son, James McConnell Smith, who was one of the first Caucasian children born west of the Blue Ridge Mountains. When his father died, James Smith took over the plantation. After taking control of the property, James became a wealthy planter and owned two plantations consisting of approximately 30,000 acres, a store, hotel, and mine.

In 1840, James Smith built a four-story Federal-style mansion as a wedding gift for his new wife, Mary Patton. Although not a plantation house in and of itself, James conducted a great deal of business concerning his two plantations from within the mansion. When his family wanted a break from plantation life, they often retreated to this mansion.

When James McConnell Smith died in 1856, his son John Patton Smith inherited the house and the rest of his father's assets. When John died the next year, his sister Sarah Lucinda Smith McDowell and her husband, William Wallace, purchased the house and the 350 acres surrounding it for $10,000. From this point, the house became known as the Smith-McDowell House.

The Smith-McDowell House has become well known for the ghosts that are said to haunt it. The most prominent ghost connected with the Smith-McDowell House is known as "the Dark One" by local residents and paranormal investigators. Investigators and visitors to the Smith-McDowell House have taken several photographs of the Dark One. Generally, this ghost is encountered near the old cistern of the mansion. Sometimes a shadowy apparition can be seen, and on more than one occasion, an image of this shadowy form has been captured on film or digital cameras. Although rare, some people even have felt the sensation of being touched or pushed when the Dark One makes an appearance.

There have been EVPs recorded of a man calling out a name as if he were searching for somebody. Some believe that the Dark One is sentient and calls out the names of people trying to communicate with him. Most believe that the Dark One is the spirit of a slave owner looking for lost slaves but that he was not a member of the Smith or McDowell families.

Another more benevolent ghost is believed to be connected to the kitchen of the Smith-McDowell House. The sound of a woman singing has been heard from the empty kitchen at all hours of the day and night. The apparition of a woman believed to be that of Mrs. James McDowell Smith is sometimes seen in conjunction with the singing.

Although not connected to the singing woman or the Dark One, there have been reports of period music heard throughout the entire house. This is generally described as piano music with no known source. The music style resembles hymns or music that was popular in the years preceding the Civil War.

STAGVILLE PLANTATION
Durham

Richard Bennehan was born in northern Virginia in 1743. When he was twenty years old, Bennehan moved to Petersburg, Virginia, to work as a merchant. Through hard work and dedication to detail, Bennehan became a well-sought-after merchant, and people would go out of their way to see him when they needed to buy supplies and other materials. In 1768 another merchant offered Bennehan a one-third partnership in a store located at a plantation in North Carolina.

Later that year, Richard Bennehan moved to North Carolina to manage the store at Snow Hill Plantation, which was located about eighteen miles from Hillsboro, North Carolina. For the next several years, Bennehan saved almost all of the money he raised and purchased 1,213 acres to establish his own plantation, which he called Bennehan Plantation. Although the actual date of construction is unknown, the two-story Georgian-style plantation house at Stagville Plantation is believed to have been built between 1787 and 1790. Through more purchases of surrounding properties, Richard Bennehan expanded his plantation to over 4,000 acres and 40 slaves by 1799.

In 1776, Richard Bennehan married Mary Amis and had two children, Rebecca and Thomas. Thomas was born in 1782 and took over the plantation when his father died in 1825. Thomas never married, but spent all of his time dedicated to the continuation of the Bennehan Plantation until his death in 1847.

Rebecca Bennehan, born in 1778, met and married Duncan Cameron, son of Reverend John Cameron, in 1803. In 1807, they moved to Stagville Plantation, which was still under the management of her brother, Thomas. After Duncan and Rebecca settled at Stagville, the Bennehan and Cameron families combined their wealth and property. Between four plantations, a mill, stores, and other land holdings from the two families, by 1860 the Bennehan and Cameron families owned over 30,000 acres and well over 900 slaves, which made it one of the largest plantation complexes of any of the Southern states.

Another building crucial to Stagville Plantation's success is the Great Barn, which was built in 1860 by slave labor. The barn was built to store mules, horses, and farming equipment used to till the land and harvest the crops on the plantation. Slaves were known to have worked at the Great Barn at all hours of the day preparing the farm equipment and mules for the fields or putting the equipment up for the evening.

From 1851 to 1860, a series of slave cabins was built near the main Bennehan House at Stagville Plantation. Collectively, these slave cabins were known as Horton Grove and are different from all of the other slave quarters in North Carolina. First, the slave quarters were two-story structures unlike slave cabins on other plantations, which were all one-story buildings. Second, the slave quarters at Horton Grove were insulated, which provided better living conditions for the slaves. As Stagville Plantation grew, so did the slave community, eventually filling Horton Grove with slave quarters constructed by the slaves themselves, most of whom had no formal education or training in carpentry.

After the Civil War, Stagville Plantation was divided and sold a number of times until the Liggett and Myers Tobacco Company acquired the plantation and much of the surrounding property. In 1976, the company donated the property to the state of North Carolina, which preserved many of the original buildings through a series of restorations. Today, Stagville Plantation is open to the public and allows visitors the opportunity to learn about the history of not only the Bennehan and Cameron families, but also what life was like on an antebellum plantation in North Carolina.

The slave quarters at Horton Grove appear to be the epicenter of the paranormal activity at Stagville Plantation, as there are at least two separate hauntings connected to the area.

The apparition of a teenage African American girl has been seen standing at the entrance of a slave cabin at Horton Grove. People who have seen this girl claim that rather than being oblivious of her surroundings, she tends to look directly at those who see her and even has taken a few steps toward them before disappearing. She has also been experienced on the second floor of the slave cabin.

Another ghost closely linked to the slave quarters may not be connected with the teenage girl. For years, people passing by the mansion and the slave quarters have claimed to have seen a small light in the upper window of both buildings. The candle-like light has been seen even when there was no electricity connected to the mansion.

Although the slave quarters are where most of the paranormal events take place, the Great Barn is also believed to be haunted. For decades, sightings have been reported of the ghost of a large adult African

American man standing or sitting in the barn's loft. People who have seen him describe him as being reclusive or frightened. It is possible that he was one of the slaves at Stagville Plantation or even a runaway slave.

Sometimes the alarm system of the Great Barn has been set off, even though nobody had been found trespassing. It has been said that on one occasion a police officer was called in to check for trespassers after an alarm at the Great Barn was triggered. When the officer went inside the Great Barn, he saw a large-built African American man. The police officer took a few steps toward the trespasser only to find him disappear in front of his eyes.

The Bennehan House also has its own share of ghostly activity, although most of what occurs inside is auditory in nature. Throughout the mansion, the sounds of footsteps and voices in conversation have been heard. Paranormal investigators have reported on various websites that they recorded EVPs of some of the voices. The mansion has also had an abundance of poltergeist activity. Furniture has been found rearranged overnight in many of the rooms, especially on the first floor of the house. Smaller items in the house have been misplaced, only to be discovered at a later time in their original locations. These events are sometimes accompanied by sudden drops in temperature of several degrees.

SEVEN

SOUTH CAROLINA

AINSLEY HALL PLANTATION/ROBERT MILLS HOUSE
Columbia

Ainsley Hall was only seventeen years old when he immigrated to America from Britain in 1800. Shortly after settling in Columbia, South Carolina, he obtained employment with a local merchant. By working with the merchant, Hall learned many tricks of the trade and after a few years he left and started a business of his own. He had saved a large amount of money and purchased a small piece of property outside of Columbia with the intent of starting his own merchandising business.

After Hall took ownership of the property, he opened Ainsley Hall and Company, which provided a variety of domestic and foreign products to customers in Columbia and surrounding communities. In addition to his business, Hall decided to start his own cotton plantation on the property. Less than ten years after opening his business and establishing his plantation, Hall acquired enough land to start five separate plantations in Chester, Fairfield, Orangeburg, Richland, and Union Counties.

In 1818, Hall commissioned renowned architect Robert Mills to build a Classic Revival mansion on the property of his first plantation. Robert Mills was the architect who designed and oversaw construction of the Washington Monument, so acquiring his services was no small task. To this day, some people refer to the mansion as the Robert Mills House rather than the Ainsley Hall Plantation House.

Although Hall spared no expense on building his mansion, he would not be fortunate enough to live in the completed structure. In August 1823, his wife, Sarah Goodwyn Hall, took a trip to New York. Hall wanted to go on the trip with her, but business kept him from doing so. Hall agreed to meet her in New York at a later time, but while en route to meet her, he fell ill and died in Virginia on August 18, 1823.

After Hall's death, the mansion was sold to a local Presbyterian church that used it as a seminary from the 1830s to the 1920s. The house served a few other purposes for the church until it was acquired in 1967 by the city of Columbia, South Carolina, to be used as a historic museum.

One ghost that is thought to haunt the Ainsley Hall Plantation House is Ainsley's wife, Sarah. She is believed to haunt the master bedroom on the second floor of the mansion. Although the house was not really used as a residence, it is believed that Sarah Hall has haunted the plantation house since her husband's death in 1823. Generally, an impression of a person lying on the bed in the room has been seen. Also, some people have claimed to see the apparition of a woman standing in the bedroom. When the apparition is described, it is consistent with an image of Sarah Hall.

BOONE HALL PLANTATION
Mt. Pleasant

In 1681, plantation owner Theophilius Patey gave 470 acres of rich farmland to his daughter and Major John Boone as a wedding gift. The property stayed in the Boone Family until it was sold to Fenwick Vardell in 1811. Vardell sold the property to John Holbock in 1817, and it remained in his family until 1935. Boone Hall exchanged hands a few more times until it was finally bought in 1955 by Harris McRae and his wife, Nancy Thomas. The couple spent two years renovating the plantation house and property before opening it to the public in 1957.

Today, the plantation is a living museum, and visitors can take tours of the mansion and several other structures that are still standing. Nine of the original slave cabins built between 1790 and 1810 and a smokehouse built in 1750 can still be toured by visitors. The most impressive original feature of Boone Hall Plantation is the beautiful three-quarter-mile Avenue of Oaks that stretches from the plantation's front gates to the plantation house itself. Records indicate that the oaks at Boone Hall Plantation were planted in 1743, and it took a century of careful cultivation to form the oak avenue that is seen today.

The Battle of Secessionville took place on June 16, 1862, on James Island about twelve miles from Mount Pleasant and Boone Hall. This battle was important in that Union troops attempted to take control of Charleston, South Carolina, but were thwarted by several Confederate soldiers. Many of these troops likely passed through Boone Hall Plantation while on their way to the battle.

In 2006, Boone Hall Farms opened a large garden where visitors can pick their own fruits and vegetables or purchase them from the local farmers' market that is on site. Boone Hall has also been the site of several television and movie projects including *The Notebook* and *North and South*. Not only has Boone Hall been featured on television shows and in cinema, but there are several events held on the property to commemorate the history of the plantation and of the town. In addition to a farmers' market and periodic events that are held at Boone Hall, a Civil War reenactment of the Battle of Secessionville takes place there on an annual basis.

Since the plantation was opened to the public in 1955, visitors have claimed to see a Union soldier bent over another fallen soldier. It looks as if the soldier is removing a bullet. The apparition is seen near where the plantation house is located. Sometimes the apparition is accompanied by a loud cry of pain.

BRICK HOUSE RUINS/
PAUL HAMILTON HOUSE
Edisto Island

Between 1708 and 1710, planter and entrepreneur Paul Hamilton purchased 470 acres from Thomas Sacheverell. The exact date that the transaction took place is unknown because any documentation referencing the exact date of the sale was lost when General Sherman and other Union officers burned down courthouses, churches, and private residences while passing through the area. This destroyed irreplaceable documentations such as deeds and property transfers.

Unlike most plantation houses, the antebellum Brick House of Edisto Island was not based on a particular architectural style, but was likely inspired by the *Cateau de la Haye d'Esquermes*, a beautiful private residence located near Loos-les-Lille in central France.

The Brick House was built in this style at the request of Paul Hamilton, original owner of the plantation. It is believed that the mansion was built between 1715 and 1725.

A unique feature of the plantation house was that it was constructed by bricks shipped in from Boston, Massachusetts, because they were denser and heavier than bricks manufactured locally. This made the mansion more structurally sound than many neighboring plantation houses. The property stayed in the Hamilton family until it was sold in 1798 to Joseph Jenkins. Since then, the property has remained in the Jenkins family.

On January 29, 1929, the plantation house burned to the ground during a wedding celebration. There was no official explanation as to the cause of the fire, although it is thought that it was caused by a careless guest who was smoking. All of the wood used in the construction of the mansion was consumed in the fire, but the front wall of the mansion that used the bricks from Boston remained standing and is still there to this day.

The ghost associated with the Brick House Ruins is that of a woman who lived there. While there is some debate as to the woman's identity, the ghost is believed to be that of Joseph Jenkins's daughter, Abigail Jenkins, who was to be married at the mansion in or around 1829.

According to a legend surrounding the Brick House, Abigail had many local men vying for her hand in marriage; they realized that the man who married Abigail also would be given the plantation to control. Knowing that the vast majority of the men were interested in her only because of the plantation, she turned all of them down. However, she fell in love with one of the suitors who appeared to have an interest in her rather than the plantation. After a short courtship, the two were engaged.

Within a few weeks, word of Abigail's engagement spread throughout Georgetown and surrounding communities, which disappointed many suitors and infuriated others. A wedding date was announced and invitations were sent to hundreds of people to attend the ceremony and reception, which was going to be held at the plantation house.

Just prior to Abigail's wedding, a rejected suitor traveled from Charleston to Edisto Island and demanded that she reconsider her decision. According to legend, when Abigail refused, he became so enraged that he drew his pistol and killed her on the spot. Some accounts of the legend claim that he killed her in front of several witnesses just moments before the ceremony was to take place.

Although the mansion no longer stands, Abigail's ghost has been seen near where the main entrance of the mansion once stood. Her apparition has been described as a young woman in her late teens or early twenties with a look of extreme sadness on her face. Photographs are also believed to exist that show a misty form near the area where she was killed.

COOLSPRING (COOL SPRINGS)

Camden

The plantation now known as Coolspring (or Cool Springs in some sources) was originally owned by John Boykin, a Camden, South Carolina, planter and attorney who owned thousands of acres of land in several counties throughout the state. In 1832, Boykin personally oversaw construction of the two-story, thirty-room Greek Revival mansion at Coolspring, which was completed two years later in 1834.

Although the plantation consisted of thousands of acres, the mansion at Coolspring was originally designed as a summer home for Boykin, whose primary residence was on another plantation several miles away.

When John Boykin died, his son Dixie Boykin inherited Coolspring and used the mansion as his primary residence. He also had some moderate success as a planter by growing several crops on site, which made it a plantation in its own right.

Dixie Boykin was known as a hard worker and a hard drinker. When not managing Coolspring, he loved to host lavish parties at the plantation. Some of these parties were said to have lasted for days at a time. However, despite his reputation of being a fun-loving and easy-going plantation owner who enjoyed a good party, all was not well in the Dixie Boykin household.

Dixie's first wife had died at a relatively young age shortly after giving birth to a daughter who became the light of her father's life. When his daughter was still fairly young, Dixie Boykin remarried and brought his new wife to Coolspring.

He loved his second wife very much, but some believe that the sentiment was not returned. Although unable to be proven, it is believed that Dixie Boykin's wife killed him or, at the very least, somehow contributed to his early demise. There may be some credence to this in that Dixie Boykin was her third husband and that her first two husbands met untimely deaths, which allowed her to make a fortune by gaining control over their respective estates.

Immediately after dinner on the evening of Dixie Boykin's death, he began to experience chest pains consistent with a heart attack. Dixie's daughter attempted to offer aid to her father, but his wife stepped in and told her that everything was under control and that her presence was upsetting her father. Reluctantly, Dixie's daughter left her father's side only to discover that he died only twenty minutes later. Some believe that Dixie Boykin's new wife poisoned him and would not allow her stepdaughter to be near him for fear that it would be discovered. The daughter was also not allowed to attend the wake or funeral for her father for fear that she might make a scene and in turn raise suspicion against her stepmother.

The ghost of Dixie Boykin makes his presence known in three separate areas of Coolspring. The first location is behind the mansion close to the rear dining room. If a person looks out the dining room window, the apparition of a man wearing a blazer can be seen walking from the fields toward the back entrance. This apparition can only be seen by looking out the dining room window. People behind the mansion or in other rooms have never reported seeing Dixie's ghost in this manner.

A second room where Dixie Boykin's ghost has been spotted is the mansion's study, in which antebellum music and other unaccounted sounds can be heard. In addition, the apparition of a man has been seen standing inside the study. The description of the man seen in the study is similar to the man seen through the dining room window. The only difference is that the man seen in the study is not wearing a blazer.

It is believed that Dixie Boykin makes his presence known at Coolspring in another way. It is rumored that, being a great connoisseur of fine spirits, Boykin had bottles of his favorite liquor or wine in each room on the first floor. This way, he would not have to carry his liquor or wine from one room to another. Today, if a wine glass is set down for a few moments in the study, dining room, or front porch, it will often be empty when the person returns to the glass. When asked, none of the guests admit to drinking or pouring out the alcohol. This has taken place for over a century and often occurs during a party or other social gathering. Legend has it that if a toast is made to Boykin and a glass is left for him, this phenomenon does not occur.

HAMPTON PLANTATION/
HAMPTON PLANTATION STATE HISTORIC SITE
McClellanville

The mansion at the Hampton Plantation is a large Georgian-style plantation house that was built in 1735 by Frederick Rutledge, a very wealthy planter who was well known in the political arena. As he was a very influential and affluent man recognized in several circles, such notable figures as George Washington were known to have been guests at the Hampton Plantation.

The oldest son of Frederick Rutledge, John Henry Rutledge, inherited the Hampton Plantation when his father died. Soon after John took over his father's estate, his mother recommended that he get married. She thought it only proper that if her son was going to take over the role of head planter at Hampton, there should be a woman of good upbringing by his side to host parties and make appearances at social gatherings when he was unable to do so.

John reluctantly agreed. After taking control of Hampton Plantation, Rutledge began to host frequent and eloquent parties for local plantation owners and members of McClellanville's upper class. Realizing the real purpose of the parties, those invited would bring their young, unmarried daughters, which gave Rutledge the opportunity to associate with them. It was no secret that many plantation owners wanted John Rutledge to marry their daughters.

After hosting several of these parties, John met and fell in love with Anna, a young and beautiful daughter of a local physician. When he realized that she loved him for who he was rather than due to the fact that he owned Hampton Plantation, they became inseparable. The relationship deepened and John decided that he wanted to have Anna as his wife.

John proposed to her and she readily accepted. John was ecstatic and immediately informed his mother, who was very critical of the news because she felt the girl was beneath a man of his standing. John became angry at his mother's interference and told her that he was in charge of Hampton Plantation and he would marry anybody he pleased. Despite his mother's advice, John continued his relationship with Anna.

John eventually asked Anna's father for her hand in marriage. Much to his surprise, the physician refused and forbade John from even associating with Anna ever again. Anna's father was in agreement with John's mother that a marriage between such different social and economic classes would be disastrous. From a young age, plantation owners' daughters were raised with the expectation of marrying another planter. This included proper training in etiquette and other social customs that somebody without proper training would be unaware of. With a heavy heart, Rutledge reluctantly ended the relationship with Anna.

John's mother convinced him to continue with the parties to find a suitable mate. Although he tried, John's heart was just not in it at all. For months, John Rutledge would make an appearance, greet his guests, and return to his bedroom. John's depression grew and he spent days on end in his bedroom, often sitting in a rocking chair for hours while looking out the window.

During a party on March 5, 1830, John Rutledge excused himself from his guests and retired to his bedroom. Knowing that this had become normal behavior for John, friends and family thought little of it. About thirty minutes later, a loud shot was heard from the vicinity of his bedroom on the second floor, which immediately put an end to all of the merriment of the party. Fearing the worst, close friends and family rushed to John's bedroom.

When his friends entered his bedroom, John was found lying on the floor in an expanding pool of blood. A pistol was in his hand, while portions of his skull and gray matter covered the floor and wall behind him. A doctor in the group noticed that John was still breathing, which was surprising considering that a large portion of his skull and brain had been destroyed in the shooting. Every effort was made to save John's life, but he never regained consciousness and died two days later as a result of complications from the shooting. After a lavish funeral, John was buried in the flower garden behind the plantation.

Shortly after John's death, family and friends began to hear the sound of a chair rocking back and forth inside the bedroom where he shot himself. When the door was opened, the rocking chair would sometimes be seen rocking on its own even though the room was empty. If the chair was placed closer to the bedroom door, it would later be found moved near the window. Sometimes, the sound of a gunshot was heard throughout the mansion. When investigated, the bedroom was always found to be empty, but the smell of gunpowder lingered in the air. People who walk in front of the house have seen the apparition of John Rutledge's ghost sitting in a chair looking out the window of his bedroom, as he was up until his suicide.

Paranormal investigators who have had the opportunity to enter the room claim to have picked up several EVP recordings, including one clear recording of a man saying, "but Anna." It is believed that this particular recording is of John Rutledge mourning over the loss of Anna, the woman he loved.

Today, Hampton Plantation is a state historic site open to visitors throughout the year. It offers people an opportunity to take tours of the mansion and other buildings that are still standing on the property. In addition, the state park offers fishing, hiking, and other outdoor activities for visitors.

HERMITAGE PLANTATION
Georgetown

Dr. Henry C. Flagg was born in Newport, Rhode Island, in 1742. After serving in the Revolutionary War as a surgeon, he moved to Charleston, where he established a plantation known as Flagg's Plantation. After retiring from practicing medicine, Dr. Flagg spent the remainder of his life maintaining his plantation.

His son, Ebenezer Flagg, was born on January 14, 1795, in Charleston and followed in his father's footsteps by becoming a well-known physician in the area. When his father died, Ebenezer took over the plantation and raised several children on it with his wife, Martha Belin Flagg.

Upon Dr. Ebenezer Flagg's death in 1838, his son, Dr. Allard Belin Flagg, inherited the plantation and became responsible for its upkeep. In 1849, as the owner of the Hermitage Plantation, Allard invited his mother, Martha, and his sixteen-year-old sister, Alice, to live with him in the main plantation house. He took his responsibilities seriously and became more of a father figure than an older brother to Alice.

A few months after settling into her new home, Alice met a local laborer about her age. They soon fell in love, even though they both knew that a courtship started between people from different societal and economic classes was frowned upon.

Dr. Allard Flagg soon learned about Alice's relationship with the laborer and forbade her from seeing him again. He said that he was trying to protect her and the family name from being tarnished. After he lectured Alice, Dr. Flagg soon confronted the boy and demanded that he never see Alice again. Dr. Flagg also told the boy that he did not want to ever see him on his property again. Heartbroken, the boy agreed and left the plantation.

Ignoring Dr. Flagg, Alice and the boy started to meet in secret and were careful not to let anybody see them together. One evening during one such meeting, the boy gave Alice a plain gold ring and told her that he wanted to marry her one day. This thrilled Alice and she immediately placed the ring upon her finger. She hugged him and snuck back to the plantation.

Unbeknownst to Alice, her brother had followed her and found out about her continued relationship with the boy. After confirming his suspicions, Dr. Flagg waited quietly one evening in Alice's bedroom for her to return from one of her meetings. When Alice sneaked back into her room, he confronted her and saw the gold ring. He immediately ordered her to take the ring off, which she did. After he left the room, Alice put the ring on a ribbon and placed it around her neck.

In order to prevent Alice and her lover from seeing each other, Dr. Flagg sent Alice to the Talvande Boarding School in Charleston, South Carolina. Reluctantly, Alice went to the boarding school but always wore the boy's ring on the ribbon around her neck.

A few months after arriving at Talvande Boarding School, Alice contracted malaria and became seriously ill. When her brother realized how sick she was, he made arrangements for her to return to the Hermitage for proper medical attention. While en route to the plantation, Alice's condition deteriorated and less than a week after returning to the Hermitage, she died.

While Alice's body was being prepared for the the funeral, the golden ring was found. Dr. Flagg became infuriated at this and threw the ring into one of the plantation's swamps. A few days later, Alice was buried in nearby All Saints Cemetery with a plain marble headstone that simply bore the name "Alice." There were no dates or surnames on the headstone at all.

In the decades since her death, people have seen Alice's ghost standing at the front of her headstone. Others have seen a similar apparition standing in front of the Hermitage as if she were waiting for somebody. There are claims that Alice has been seen walking near the plantation's swamps. It is believed that she is looking in vain for the golden ring that her brother threw into the swamp after she died. Today, if a person visits the cemetery and finds Alice's gravestone, it is not uncommon to see several rings and flowers given as an offering to her.

Today, the property of Hermitage Plantation is used as a private housing community and golf course. Although it does have a historical significance and there are legends associated with its haunting, please keep in mind that the Hermitage is private property and cannot be visited without permission. However, the All Saints Episcopal Church graveyard where Alice is buried is still accessible to the public. Her grave is still marked with the tombstone that simply reads "Alice." As it is located near a church, please approach the cemetery with respect.

LITCHFIELD PLANTATION
Pawleys Island

In 1710, Thomas Hepworth was given 500 acres of land near present-day Georgetown, South Carolina. By 1713, Thomas Hepworth had acquired a total of 1,420 acres through a series of land grants given to him by the British Crown, and he cultivated the property into a very prosperous plantation.

In 1740, local businessman Peter Simon bought the entire plantation from Thomas Hepworth. Immediately after taking ownership, Simon constructed the original antebellum plantation house on the land. He was also the man who first referred to the property as Litchfield.

Upon Simon's death on November 10, 1794, his two sons inherited Litchfield. One son had very little interest in running a plantation and in 1796 sold his share of the plantation to Daniel Tucker. When Daniel Tucker died, he passed the property to his oldest son, John Tucker, who in turn passed it on to his oldest son, Dr. Henry Tucker.

Dr. Henry Tucker was a compassionate and talented physician in the Georgetown area. He was said to have been so dedicated to his patients that he would travel on horseback to make a house call at all hours of the night. When Dr. Tucker realized that this would become a regular occurrence, he arranged for a house servant to wait by the back gate where a large iron bell had been placed. When Dr. Tucker returned from one of his house calls, he rang the bell to alert the servant of his arrival. The servant then opened the gate and put the horse into its stall. Meanwhile, Dr. Tucker quietly sneaked up a back set of stairs so as to not wake his family.

For years, Dr. Tucker worked with local residents and tried to help them whenever he could. His compassion for others continued until his death in 1897. After his death, Litchfield was sold out of the Tucker family and has exchanged hands several times since then.

The ghost associated with Litchfield Plantation is that of Dr. Henry Tucker. On some nights, the sound of a horse galloping can be heard near where the original gate used to stand. The sound of a ringing bell can also be heard at the same location, although the bell that Dr. Tucker used to signal his servant was removed shortly after his death.

In addition to the activity at the gate, the sound of heavy footsteps has been heard on the back staircase to the second floor, where Dr. Tucker's bedroom was located. At times, the sound is accompanied by the apparition of a weary man in his late thirties who ascends the staircase from the ground floor to the second floor.

A similar apparition has been seen in what is known as the Blue Room, which was Dr. Tucker's old bedroom. The apparition is seen either standing in the doorway facing into the bedroom or at the window looking out onto the lawn below.

MAGNOLIA PLANTATION AND GARDENS
Charleston

Magnolia Plantation was founded by Thomas Drayton in 1679. As the owner of one of the oldest rice plantations in North America, Drayton made a fortune by being a producer of rice long before many of the other plantations in the state even existed. For over three hundred years, Magnolia Plantation remained in the Drayton family.

Thomas Drayton's great-grandson, Thomas Drayton IV, died in 1825 but did not have any biological sons to pass Magnolia Plantation to.

He did have two grandsons through his youngest daughter. The grandsons' names were Thomas and John Grimke.

Just prior to his death, Thomas Drayton IV made a deal with the two brothers. He would give them Magnolia Plantation and all of the wealth associated with it if they would legally change their names from Grimke to Drayton. Without hesitation, John and Thomas agreed to do so.

John and Thomas Drayton were two very different men with considerably different personalities. Realizing that his older brother Thomas would likely be in charge of the plantation for years, John traveled abroad and enjoyed a carefree lifestyle. He was content that his older brother controlled the plantation, because he had no interest in having anything to do with it at all.

While John was traveling in England, Thomas was killed in a hunting accident on the plantation. When John learned of his brother's death, he returned to take care of Magnolia Plantation. John was only twenty-two years old at the time and soon learned that there was a great deal to being the owner of a plantation.

After putting all of his brother's affairs in order, John entered the ministry. While he had obligations to Magnolia, John moved from South Carolina to New York and entered an Episcopal seminary in 1838. While in the seminary, John met and married Julia Ewing, the daughter of a wealthy attorney from Philadelphia. Shortly after they were married, John convinced Julia to move to South Carolina to help him manage Magnolia Plantation.

Upon their return to Magnolia, John built a large and beautiful botanical garden for Julia. He wanted to make certain his wife would appreciate South Carolina's natural beauty. Also, while in seminary, John had developed tuberculosis, which weakened him physically. He thought that working on a botanical garden would not only please Julia, but that the fresh air and focusing on his garden would help to return him to health.

A few years after returning with his wife to Magnolia, John became the rector of the Saint Andrews Church, a small church founded in 1709 and located less than four miles from Magnolia Plantation. John was rector to the church for fifty years until his death.

While not running the plantation or being in the service of God, John spent his free time working on the botanical garden. Within a few years, the garden gained international attention. Among other botanical milestones connected to Magnolia Plantation, John was the man responsible for introducing azaleas to North America.

In 1870, Magnolia Plantation was opened to the public for tours of the botanical gardens. Today, the Magnolia Plantation and Gardens still offers tours of the property and provides a detailed history of the plantation. It also happens to have some ghost stories that have gained a great deal of attention.

Magnolia Plantation was the focus of the *Ghost Hunters* episode "Paranormal Politics" (episode 18 of the eighth season). During the episode, several EVPs were recorded, including the sound of music, a cough, and a voice of a young girl or woman asking, "What are you doing?"

The Oaks Plantation
Saint Helena Island

The property near Murrells Inlet, South Carolina, that would become the Oaks Plantation was acquired by Deputy Governor Robert Daniell through a land grant. Daniell sold the property to Joseph Allston in 1730. The original plantation house was built not long after Allston purchased the property. In 1760, Allston built a second plantation house before giving the property to his son William Alston, who in turn bequeathed the property to his son, future governor of South Carolina Joseph Alston.

The Oaks Plantation owner Governor Joseph Alston married Theodosia Burr on February 2, 1801, in Albany, New York. Not only was the trip their honeymoon, but there was also a scheduled stop in

Washington, DC, to see Theodosia's father, Aaron Burr, be inaugurated as Thomas Jefferson's vice president. After their wedding, Joseph brought Theodosia home to the Oaks Plantation.

In 1802, Theodosia gave birth to her only child, Aaron Burr Alston, named after her father. The pregnancy was difficult for Theodosia, and after her son was born, she was very weak for several months. Being from New York, Theodosia often took retreats to one of her favorite locations, the Ballston Spa in Saratoga, New York.

During the summer of 1806, Theodosia and her son were invited to meet with her father on Blennerhassett Island on the Ohio River, right outside of present-day Parkersburg, West Virginia. She only stayed a short time on Blennerhassett Island before she returned to the Oaks Plantation. Little did she know that Harman Blennerhassett and Aaron Burr, with the help of General James Wilkinson, were making plans for a succession of Louisiana and parts of the western United States to form their own country.

Due to his dealings with Harman Blennerhassett and General James Wilkinson, Aaron Burr was arrested for treason and extradited for trial in Richmond, Virginia. Always supportive of her father, Theodosia was there for him throughout the trial. Burr was acquitted of the treason charge, but immediately after the hearing he moved to Europe and lived there for four years. He would have likely stayed in Europe had it not been for a tragedy that Theodosia experienced in the summer of 1812.

Joseph Alston's father, William, had purchased a beautiful stretch of property on DeBordieu Beach, not far from the main plantation house of the Oaks. Upon purchasing the property, Alston built a summer house that overlooked DeBordieu Beach and the waves of the Atlantic Ocean. After the retreat was built, it became known as the Castle.

Between 1812 and 1814, Joseph Alston was extremely busy with not just the Oaks Plantation but also as South Carolina's forty-fourth governor. The obligations of such an office prevented Joseph from being with his family for long periods of time. However, he did try to be there for his family as time permitted.

During the late spring of 1812, Joseph, Theodosia, and their ten-year-old son, Aaron, would often be found at the Castle. When Joseph's responsibilities as governor called him away from the Oaks, Theodosia would take Aaron to the Castle for days on end. She found the ocean waves near the Castle particularly soothing.

Early in the summer of 1812, Aaron became very ill from complications of contracting malaria. Joseph took Theodosia and Aaron to stay permanently at the Castle in an effort to help him recover from the disease. Sadly, Aaron Burr Alston passed away on June 30, 1812, at the Castle with his parents by his side.

After Aaron's death, Theodosia went into a very deep depression. She isolated herself from her family and refused to speak with any friends who came by to visit. She spent virtually all of her time at the Castle, often walking in solitude along DeBordieu Beach.

Word soon got to Aaron Burr about his grandson's death and his daughter's depression. He immediately returned to New York City and made arrangements to meet her later in the year. As it had been years since she had seen her father, Theodosia agreed to visit with him. Arrangements were made to charter a schooner known as *The Patriot* to sail from Georgetown, South Carolina, to New York City in early 1813.

Joseph Alston escorted Theodosia to *The Patriot* to see her off. Due to business and political obligations, Joseph was unable to accompany Theodosia to New York. However, he did arrange for long-time family friend Dr. Timothy Green to accompany Theodosia on the ten-day voyage from Georgetown to New York. As Joseph watched *The Patriot* sail into the distance, he had no idea that it would be the last time that he would ever see his wife.

The Patriot left port in Georgetown, South Carolina, on December 31, 1812, but never arrived to its destination in New York City. Although search parties were formed, no wreckage of the schooner was ever found. After weeks of searching, Theodosia, Dr. Green, and the rest of the passengers and crew were declared lost at sea. Speculation of their fate ranged from a pirate attack to being caught by an unexpected storm off of Cape Fear, North Carolina.

As Theodosia's body was never recovered, a monument was erected next to her son's grave in the family graveyard. Due to the loss of his wife and son, Joseph vowed never to marry again. He died alone in 1816 when he was only thirty-seven years old and is buried next to his family in the graveyard.

The Oaks has three separate hauntings attributed to Theodosia. Near the dock in Georgetown from which *The Patriot* embarked, the ghost of a woman has been seen standing on the beach looking out over the ocean. When this ghost is seen, she is described as a young woman with long straight hair and wearing a light-colored dress. Some locals believe that if Theodosia's ghost is seen at the docks, it is an omen that there may be an approaching storm or that some tragic event is about to occur.

Near the site of the Castle, the apparition of a woman believed to be Theodosia Alston has been seen walking along DeBordieu Beach. This ghost is almost identical to the apparition seen at the Georgetown docks. The main differences between the two ghosts is that this apparition wears a darker dress and rather than standing in one place, she is seen walking along the beach in much the same way that she did in the months following her son's death.

Although these two ghosts have been seen at the Castle and the Georgetown docks, Theodosia has also been seen at two separate locations at the Oaks Plantation itself. She has been seen standing in front of the main entrance of the plantation house and in the family graveyard located close to the mansion. When she is seen in the graveyard, it appears that she is looking for something. It is possible that she may be searching for either her own grave or the grave of her son.

STONEY-BAYNARD PLANTATION/BAYNARD RUINS/ BRADDOCK'S POINT PLANTATION

Hilton Head Island

In 1774, twenty-four-year-old Captain Jack Stoney and his wife, Elizabeth, immigrated to Hilton Head, South Carolina, from Tipperary, Ireland. Two years later, Captain Stoney purchased a 1,000-acre tract of land on the island known to locals as Braddock's Point.

In 1793, Captain Stoney constructed a medium-sized plantation house for his family. Rather than use an architectural style common among Southern plantation houses, Stoney built his home from a material known as tabby, which is a mixture of sand, lime, oyster shells, and water. The primary crop of the plantation was sea island cotton, which was commonly grown on coastal antebellum plantations.

Captain Stoney kept the plantation at Braddock's Point in good order until he died in an unexpected hunting accident in 1821. Upon his death, the plantation was equally divided between his two sons, James and John Stoney.

Being the oldest, James maintained control of Braddock's Point until his death in 1827. After James's death, John inherited the plantation and attempted to keep it afloat for several years until he died in 1838, heavily in debt.

Another well-known planter in the area was Thomas Baynard, who was one of the largest landowners and richest men in the Hilton Head area. Baynard and his wife, Sarah, had four sons: John, Archibald, Ephram, and William. John Baynard died at a young age, Arichbald made a name for himself in South Carolina politics, Ephram became South Carolina's first millionnaire, and William Baynard became a very successful planter and investor.

Following his father's death, William Baynard inherited the 600-acre Spanish Wells Plantation, which was located near the Braddock's Point Plantation. Soon he expanded his holdings to include the 850-acre Muddy Creek Plantation and a several-hundred-acre property known as Buckingham Plantation. Baynard made a fortune by actively searching for and purchasing plantations that were struggling financially. By the time he was thirty years old, William Baynard was in control of at least three separate plantations totaling several thousand acres, which made him one of the largest property owners in the area. Soon he added Braddock's Point to his list of properties owned.

There was a widely circulated rumor that John Stoney lost Braddock's Point in a poker game with William Baynard. This was not the case, as there is paperwork documenting that Baynard purchased Braddock's Point from the Bank of Charleston on December 17, 1845, for $10,000.

After Baynard settled into the plantation house at Braddock's Point, locals began referring to the property as Baynard Hall or the Stoney-Baynard House. Unfortunately, William Baynard did not get a chance to stay at his home at Braddock's Point for very long. He died unexpectedly at the plantation house on May 2, 1849, when he was forty-nine years old. He left behind his seven children and his wife, who was in her fifth month of pregnancy with their eighth child.

For Baynard's funeral, the family mausoleum he had built years earlier at the Zion Chapel of Ease Cemetery was prepared to receive him. A large black-draped wagon served as the hearse, which was followed from the mansion to the Chapel of Ease, where the funeral service was conducted by Reverend Alsop Woodward. To show their respect, plantation owners in attendance brought hundreds of slaves to line the roads leading to the chapel. To this day, it is believed that William Baynard's funeral was the largest ever to have taken place upon the island.

William's son Ephram took over and managed Braddock's Point well into the Civil War. On November 7, 1863, Ephram and his family were forced from Baynard Hall when over 12,000 Union troops took control of the area.

At some point between August and December 1867, the plantation house was burned. Although it has been thought that decommissioned

Union soldiers intentionally burned it, some believe that the abandoned mansion was burned by trespassers. Although Ephram Baynard returned to the property for a short time in 1868, he never tried to rebuild the mansion.

For nearly two hundred years, there have been ghost stories connected to the Stoney-Baynard Plantation House, including several accounts of encounters with Baynard, his family, and Union soldiers stationed on the island.

Grave robbery was not an unheard of crime during the years following the Civil War. After the Confederate States of America was dissolved and Reconstruction was underway, the economy of the Southern states was in complete shambles. As a result, some people robbed graves and mausoleums of wealthy families in order to find rings, necklaces, and other valuables that may have been buried with them.

According to legend, on one night shortly after Baynard Hall was burned in 1867, two men attempted to rob Baynard Mausoleum. Shortly after breaking into the outer chamber, one robber was hit in the head by a section of ceiling that collapsed, killing him instantly.

The second robber reached the inner vault where the bodies of William Baynard and his wife lay. Before he could desecrate William's remains, the large door connecting the inner and outer chambers slammed shut. Unable to open the door from the inside, and with his lantern burning itself out, the man slowly died from lack of oxygen in complete darkness. Some people believe that it was the ghost of William Baynard protecting his family's remains from being desecrated.

By the mid-1950s, the ruins and mausoleum had become a favorite hangout for teenagers living on the island. Another ghost story associated with the mausoleum emerged during this time. According to some teenagers, the sound of a man crying for help has been heard from deep within Baynard Mausoleum, even though the doors are no longer standing and the remains of the Baynards have been moved. It may be the ghost of the grave robber who was sealed alive inside the mausoleum.

Since Baynard's death, a large funeral procession consisting of a large black horse-drawn hearse, followed by several black carriages, has been seen traveling from the ruins of Baynard Hall to the family mausoleum. As the procession nears the mausoleum, it disappears. The carriages are sometimes accompanied by the faint outlines of men and women standing on either side of the road. These are likely the ghosts of slaves brought to the island for the service by plantation owners paying their respects to William Baynard.

While not directly related to Baynard's Hall, there is another legend associated with Hilton Head Island and Braddock's Point. During the Revolutionary War, British soldiers sometimes sneaked onto coastal plantations and kidnapped slaves. They would then abandon the slaves on one the many barrier islands surrounding Hilton Head. The slaves were unable to return to the mainland and died from either starvation, dehydration, or drowning. The rationale was that the plantation owner would have to spend a great deal of money to replace the lost slaves or lose a great deal of income from not being able to harvest crops. There have been sightings of British soldiers on the shores of the island. Sometimes they are accompanied by the cries of people coming from the direction of the barrier islands.

THOMAS ROSE HOUSE
Charleston

The Thomas Rose House is named after planter Thomas Rose, who built the two-and-a-half-story Georgian-style mansion between 1735 and 1740. After Rose's death, the entire plantation was given to his widow, who soon sold the property. The property exchanged hands several times until it was finally purchased by Dr. Joseph Ladd Brown.

Dr. Brown was originally a resident of Rhode Island until he visited Charleston, South Carolina, for business. While in Charleston, Dr. Brown fell in love with the area and immediately decided to relocate. While looking for property to purchase, he found that the Thomas Rose House and surrounding property was for sale. Without hesitation, Dr.

Brown immediately purchased the property and proceeded to move to Charleston, South Carolina.

In Charleston, Dr. Brown resumed his medical practice and became a well-respected resident of the area. During his free time, he frequently socialized with others and participated in local social events; he especially enjoyed going to live performances held in a well-known theater hall in Charleston.

After attending a Shakespearean play at the theater one evening, Dr. Brown criticized the acting ability of an actress in the performance. His comments infuriated one of the gentlemen he was speaking with and soon the two were engaged in a very heated argument. The gentleman challenged Dr. Brown to a duel with pistols the following day. Dr. Brown did not wish to be perceived as a coward in front of many of Charleston's most influential residents, so he reluctantly agreed to the challenge.

The next morning arrived and the hour of the duel approached. Dr. Brown realized that the honor of a woman he never met was not worth dueling over and attempted to talk with his opponent about canceling the duel, but he soon discovered that this was not an option. Dr. Brown decided that rather than shoot his opponent, he would fire his weapon into the air and forfeit the duel. Dr. Brown did so, believing that his challenger would not shoot an unarmed man.

The man walked up to Dr. Brown, who thought that he was approaching him to call the duel a draw. Dr. Brown extended his right arm to shake hands with his challenger. Rather than accept this gesture, the man fired his pistol at point-blank range into Dr. Brown's kneecap, literally destroying it. Dr. Brown immediately fell to the ground in agony. The challenger then ruthlessly shot Dr. Brown in the other kneecap while he was lying on the ground.

As the injury took place during a duel, which was legal at the time, Dr. Brown's opponent was not charged with any crime. Unable to walk, Dr. Brown was carried to his bedroom in the Thomas Rose

House, where he died three weeks later of complications due to infection and gangrene.

There are at least two separate ghosts that haunt the Thomas Rose House. The ghost most frequently encountered at the house is of Dr. Joseph Brown, who has been seen standing on the lawn in front of the mansion where the duel took place. As Dr. Brown's apparition has sometimes been accompanied by the sound of a person whistling, he has become known as the Whistling Ghost of the Thomas Rose House.

Another ghost connected to the Thomas Rose House is that of a little girl who died there in the 1830s. The girl has been described as eight to ten years old and can be seen and heard in a room on the first floor of the plantation house. Her ghost has also been seen playing behind the plantation house.

WEDGEFIELD PLANTATION

Georgetown

Although the actual year that Wedgefield Plantation was established is unknown, records indicate that it was producing crops before 1750. Although not the largest plantation in comparison to others, the fact that Wedgefield was established so long ago makes it one of the oldest existing plantations in the entire state of South Carolina.

Wedgefield was originally owned and operated by John Green, who owned at least four other plantations throughout South Carolina. In 1762, planter Samuel Wragg purchased Wedgefield Plantation and one of the first things that Wragg did was build a much larger plantation house and convert Green's original plantation house into the plantation overseer's residence.

During the Revolutionary War, Wragg attempted to remain neutral in the conflict between the Colonists and the British. Although he longed for independence and sided with the Colonists, the British were some of his best customers and accounted for a vast majority of his financial success. He knew that if he refused to do business with them, it would ruin him financially. He also realized that he could make even more money if he provided information about the Colonists' plans to them.

As hostilities between the British and Colonists escalated, it was discovered that Wragg was covertly working with British troops and appeared to support their cause. In all actuality, Wragg was only interested in making money from them. Virtually everybody in Wragg's life, with the exception of his daughter, abandoned him. They would not socialize with him or buy any of his goods and soon Wragg's only customers were the British.

Wragg's daughter was also in favor of independence and realized that she was in the prime position to help the Colonists because of her father's involvement with the British. She stayed by her father and befriended many of the British officers that frequently visited Wedgefield.

As was common with Union and Confederate troops during the Civil War, British and Colonial troops often commandeered houses, barns, and other buildings for their respective causes. Most often, they used them as field hospitals or headquarters. However, in some cases, they used them as prisoner-of-war camps. Wedgefield was used as a POW camp for high-ranking Colonial prisoners. At any given point, there were between ten and fifteen prisoners who were guarded by up to twenty armed British soldiers.

It was believed that one high-ranking Colonial official in particular was imprisoned at Wedgefield. As Wragg's daughter still had access to the plantation, she confirmed this and passed this information to the Colonists. The particular prisoner was privy to sensitive intelligence that pertained to Colonists' plans, locations of troops and fortifications, and other confidential information. The problem with this particular prisoner was that he was starting to show early signs of dementia, and could unintentionally provide sensitive information to his captors at any time. The Colonists knew that he needed to be extracted from the site, but also knew that a frontal assault would be tragic.

Wragg's daughter came up with the idea of hosting a formal dinner at nearby Mansfield Plantation in honor of the British soldiers, their families, and a select number of loyalists. The British officers agreed and soon the dinner party was planned. The night of the party, the prisoners at Wedgefield were guarded by only one young British soldier. It was assumed that he could manage by himself for a few hours.

A small group of Colonial troops snuck up on the guard and surrounded him as he stood in front of the mansion. The British soldier stood his ground and fired at his assailants. The shot missed a calvaryman, who drew his sword and swiftly decapitated the British soldier in one stroke. Rather than falling to the ground, the body staggered a few steps and spewed blood in all directions before falling next to its own severed head. In the journals of men who were present, most wrote that it was the most disturbing image that they had seen in all of their years on the battlefield. With the guard out of the way, the Colonists were able to release all of the prisoners without incident.

With such a history, there are several ghost stories associated with Wedgefield Plantation. One of the most lasting stories connected to Wedgefield is that of the decapitated British soldier. Although the mansion was torn down in the 1930s, for decades there have been eyewitness accounts of a headless British soldier seen staggering a few steps before collapsing to the ground and disappearing.

Although the headless British soldier is the most well-known ghost, there are accounts of another haunting that takes place near where the original Wedgefield Plantation House once stood. A second unidentified British soldier has been seen standing at attention where the entrance of the original plantation house was located. Although both apparitions associated with this plantation are of British soldiers, it is not believed that the two ghosts seen are the same soldier. The soldier standing at attention is also sometimes accompanied by the sound of gunfire and the gallop of horse hooves, whereas the decapitated soldier does not have this.

— EIGHT —

VIRGINIA

ABIJAH THOMAS HOUSE/OCTAGONAL HOUSE
Marion

When Abijah Thomas built a mansion on his plantation near Marion, Virginia, he decided to take a different route than many other planters in the area. Unlike many plantation houses throughout Virginia, Thomas's mansion was octagonal, which was loosely based on the Jeffersonian architectural style. In the 1850s, octagonal structures were starting to become somewhat popular, but never reached the demand of more traditional architectural styles such as Federal or Greek Revival. In addition to the Abijah Thomas House, the most well-known octagonal mansion would be Longwood in Natchez, Mississippi. Once the Civil War began, the interest in constructing octagonal mansions diminished considerably.

The Abijah Thomas House had seventeen full-size rooms, ten closets, and a large storage room known to locals as the Dark Room. Although Thomas was a moderately successful planter with a fairly easy-going demeanor, rumors spread that he was cruel to his slaves. It had been said that Thomas occasionally went into intense rages and took his anger out on any slave who happened to be nearby. According to some accounts, Thomas would take slaves to the storage room and beat them. Although there does not appear to be any documentation to support this, if what the locals said is true, it is understandable why the storage room got the name of the Dark Room.

The Dark Room has become known as the most haunted part of the Abijah Thomas House. Screams have been heard coming from inside the Dark Room. When a person enters the room and attempts to find the source of the screaming, it abruptly ceases. Some paranormal investigators have claimed to have recorded these screams as EVPs. Sometimes a sense of overwhelming despair has been felt when a person enters the room. There have also been a large number of photographs taken in the Dark Room that contain misty forms or orbs in the images.

Unlike many of the other plantation houses in this book, the Abijah Thomas House has not fared well over the years. After Thomas's death, the house was abandoned and fell into a state of disrepair. Although the Abijah Thomas House was placed on the National Register of Historic Places in November 1980, little has been done to renovate the mansion into its former condition.

The plantation house can be found on a country road not far from Marion, Virginia. The plantation house is not structurally sound, so it is not advisable to enter the building, which can be seen from the road.

APPOMATTOX MANOR
Hopewell

Captain Francis Eppes purchased a parcel of land near the current location of Hopewell, Virginia, in 1635 to start a small plantation of his own. With each generation, the size of the plantation increased, and by the mid-1800s, the size of Appomattox was approximately 2,300 acres and was taken care of by more than 120 slaves.

At the onset of the Civil War, Francis Eppes's great-grandson, Dr. Richard Eppes, lived on the plantation with his family. Although Richard Eppes tried to maintain control of his property, he and his family were removed from their home in 1862 by Union forces, who took over the plantation house. Dr. Eppes left behind nearly all of his belongings and was only able to take some clothing and other small personal belongings. As for Dr. Eppes's slaves, it was said that just prior to leaving his plantation, he released all of them. After moving to several locations, Eppes eventually became a surgeon at a Confederate hospital in Pennsylvania for the remainder of the Civil War.

Once the mansion was abandoned by Dr. Eppes, Union Quartermaster Rufus Ingalls used the mansion as his field headquarters, with hundreds of Union soldiers staying on the surrounding acreage. The mansion and property remained in the possession of the Union army for the remainder of the Civil War.

After the Civil War ended, Eppes and his family returned to Appomattox only to find that the mansion was unlivable and most of the property all but destroyed.

In regards to hauntings, there is one legend associated with Appomattox. According to some sources, there was a nurse who tended a Union soldier who had life-threatening wounds. Although she attempted to help him, his injuries were too severe and he soon died. His body was taken to the basement of the plantation house, unbeknownst to anybody but the nurse. The story is that nearly a century later, the soldier's skeletal remains were found in the basement and that after the remains were moved, his apparition, along with other paranormal activity, started to transpire. This usually consisted of the sound of scrapings, voices, and similar noises coming from the basement near where the soldier's corpse was found.

AVENEL HOUSE/
WILLIAM M. BURWELL HOUSE
Bedford

The William M. Burwell House, also known as the Avenel House, in Bedford, Virginia, is a large Federal and Greek Revival-style mansion built in 1838 by William Burwell as a wedding gift to his bride, Frances

Steptoe. In addition to the mansion, several adjacent buildings, including a smokehouse and a barn, were built. Today, the site is open to the public, can be reserved for weddings and other events, and hosts several fundraising events each year.

An interesting fact about Avenel is that General Robert E. Lee and his family had a very close relationship with the Burwells before the start of the Civil War, which continued until Lee's death in 1870. Letita Burwell wrote about how the Lees and Burwells became acquainted and the lifelong friendship that followed in her memoir, *A Girl's Life in Virginia Before the War*.

In 1863, Robert E. Lee's wife had become very ill and it was recommended that she find a quiet place in the country to rest and regain her health. Lee took it upon himself to write letters to dozens of plantation owners in hopes that she could stay with them for for a short time.

After receiving Lee's letter, Mrs. Burwell immediately wrote back and invited them to stay at Avenel as long as they wanted. They accepted the offer and Mrs. Lee spent several weeks at the plantation. Through the course of her visit, the Burwells and Lees became very good friends.

Although no major tragedies are believed to have taken place at the Burwell House, some say that it may be one of the most haunted places in the Bedford, Virginia, area, as there are at least three distinct hauntings associated with the mansion.

The most frequently reported haunting at the Burwell House is of a ghost that has become known as the Lady in White. It is believed that the Lady in White is actually the ghost of William Burwell's wife, Frances Steptoe Burwell. Her silent apparition is often seen descending the main staircase leading to the mansion's entryway. Frances's ghost is described as a younger woman wearing either a white bridal gown or a light-colored evening dress.

Perhaps the most famous haunting at Burwell Plantation is not the Lady in White but the Burwell family pet. For several years, visitors who have entered the mansion's parlor claim that they felt a cat rubbing up against their ankles. This sensation is often accompanied by a loud purr. When the visitor would look down to pet or pick up the cat, there is no cat to be seen. The sound of loud purring and meows have been picked up as EVPs, although there were no living cats in the mansion when the recording was made.

One of the rooms at the William Burwell House has become known as the Lee Room. When Lee and his wife visited the Burwells, they always stayed in the same guest room. When the mansion was opened to the public for tours, this bedroom was named the Lee Room in acknowledgment of this fact. Both staff and visitors have claimed to notice an impression on the bed, as if somebody is still lying down in it.

In addition to the three ghosts at the Burwell House, there have been reports of whispering voices, loud footsteps, and other unexplained sounds. Many of these sounds have been recorded as EVPs by ghost hunters who have been fortunate enough to investigate the Burwell House.

BELLE GROVE PLANTATION
Middletown

Soon after Isaac Hite Sr. moved to the Middletown, Virginia, area, he purchased 300 acres on which to cultivate a plantation. It was moderately successful, and twenty-two years later, he purchased an additional 183 acres adjacent to the original property.

In 1783, Isaac Hite Sr. gave the entire plantation to his son Isaac Hite Jr. as a wedding gift to him and his new bride, Nelly Conway Madison, who was President James Madison's sister.

Immediately after inheriting the nearly 500-acre plantation, Isaac Hite Jr. began construction of a large mansion for himself and his wife. The mansion was built between 1794 and 1797 in the Federal architectural style.

Isaac Hite Jr. developed a strong friendship with his brother-in-law, President James Madison. Some believe that Madison may have been influential in convincing Hite to choose the Federal architectural style for his plantation house. According to records, James Madison had such an affinity for his brother-in-law, his sister, and Belle Grove that he spent his honeymoon on the property.

Over the years, Hite was able to purchase additional acreage until he had a total of 7,500 acres and 103 slaves to tend to the property. He also expanded his business to include a general store, a sawmill, and a distillery. Although Hite was fairly successful as a planter and business-man, there was one tragedy at the plantation that affected him until his death in 1836.

The smokehouse at Belle Grove was the site of a gruesome mur-der that took place in 1802. In the late 1700s, Hite took on a slave girl named Millie as one of his mistresses. He arranged for her to move into the house to assist with domestic chores and to be closer to him. His wife, Nelly, soon discovered the affair and demanded that Millie be returned to the fields. A few days later, Hite had to go to town for business but agreed to take care of the problem upon his return.

Realizing that she would have to return to field work, Millie de-vised a plan to kill Nelly. With her out of the way, Millie thought that she could take her place and become Hite's second wife. However, Millie knew she had to act fast and make Nelly's death appear like an accident.

When Hite was in town on business, Millie saw it as the perfect opportunity to murder Nelly. Millie came to Nelly hysterical and told her that there was something she needed to see in the smokehouse. Once Nelly and Millie were alone in the smokehouse, Millie attacked her from behind with a blunt object, fracturing her skull and breaking several bones. Realizing what she had done, Millie panicked and left Nelly for dead. By the time Hite returned and found his wife, Millie had already fled the plantation, never to be seen again.

Today, the sound of two women fighting can be heard from within the smokehouse. There have also been people who claimed to have heard a weak moaning from the inside of the mansion. Sometimes this is accompanied by the smell of smoking wood.

Another ghost is said to haunt Belle Grove. The Hites had three children, but one daughter died when she was only five years old. After her funeral, Hite buried her in the family graveyard. Since her death, the apparition of a little girl has been seen sitting in front of one of the graves.

BERKELEY PLANTATION
Charles City

Berkeley Plantation was built upon the site of a settlement known as Berkeley Hundred, which was one of the first settlements to be established in the New World. The settlement was attacked on March 22, 1622, by Opchancanough, tribal chief of the Powhatan Confederacy. He coordinated a simultaneous attack on several settlements in the Virginia Colony, including Berkeley Hundred. Nine settlers died in the raid on Berkeley Hundred. Realizing that they were outnumbered, survivors of the attack fled to Jamestown, Virginia, and the settlement was abandoned.

Several years later, William Tucker purchased the property on which Berkeley Hundred was situated. After owning the property for several years, Tucker sold Berkeley Plantation to John Bland. When Bland died, ownership of the plantation went to his son, Giles Bland, who had been involved with Bacon's Rebellion. The short-lived and unsuccessful Bacon's Rebellion was an attempt to forcibly remove Virginia governor William Berkeley from office.

During an unrelated event, Bland was arrested and brought before Governor Berkeley, who recognized him and had him hanged for his involvement with Bacon's Rebellion. After Giles Bland's death, Governor Berkeley took ownership of the property. In 1691, he sold the property to Benjamin Harrison III, who used his newly purchased property to build the first commercial shipyard on the James River to export tobacco grown on his plantations.

When Benjamin Harrison III died in 1710, his son, Benjamin Harrison IV, inherited the nearly 1,000-acre parcel of land. When he took ownership of the land, he built a three-story Georgian-style plantation house on the site in 1726. Today, the plantation house is one of the oldest standing brick mansions in Virginia.

Berkeley Plantation was influential in the early days of our nation's history. The first Thanksgiving celebration took place on the land in 1619. The first bourbon whiskey was distilled on the property in 1621. In July 1862, "Taps" was played for the first time ever at Berkeley. Two United States presidents, William Harrison and Benjamin Harrison, lived at Berkeley Plantation at one point.

Although Berkeley has had its share of historical milestones, it has also had its share of tragedies since the mid-1700s that may have led to some of the hauntings that can still be experienced today.

During a thunderstorm in the summer of 1745, an upstairs bedroom window of the mansion blew open and heavy rain poured in, threatening to destroy the bedroom's expensive furniture. Benjamin Harrison IV and his two daughters were in the room and ran to the window to close it when a large bolt of lightning struck the house, immediately killing all three of them.

After his father's unexpected death, Benjamin Harrison V became caretaker of Berkeley Plantation, which was quite an undertaking, considering he was only eighteen years old. However, he not only successfully managed the plantation for several years, but he was also a signer of the Declaration of Independence, the governor of Virginia, and father of President Henry Harrison and great-grandfather of President William Henry Harrison.

The Civil War found the Harrison family no longer residing at the plantation. General George McClellan and as many as 10,000 Union troops were stationed at Berkeley. General McClellan occupied the mansion while Union soldiers were spread throughout the plantation's 1,000 acres. Because of its proximity to Washington, D.C., President

Abraham Lincoln personally visited General McClellan at Berkeley Plantation on at least two occasions during the Civil War.

While he was at Berkeley Plantation, General McClellan converted the mansion's cellar into a holding cell for captured Confederate soldiers. Often the captured soldiers were harshly interrogated while imprisoned in the cellar. Many of the bedrooms of the mansion were also transformed into hospital rooms for wounded Union soldiers when they returned from the battlefield. Undoubtedly, many Confederate soldiers met their fate as a result of their stay in the cellar and many Union soldiers died in the bedrooms of the mansion.

After the Civil War ended, many of the Harrisons attempted to return to Berkeley Plantation but were unable to do so. Again, the property was abandoned and left to the elements for several years. James Jamieson, a Civil War veteran of Scottish descent, purchased the property in 1907 and spent months renovating the mansion to its former splendor. Today, the Berkeley Plantation House is a historical landmark that offers tours of the mansion and hosts several community events throughout the year. It can also be reserved for weddings and other special events.

With a history that has spanned four hundred years, the land and the mansion are believed to have several ghosts associated with them. Interestingly enough, most of the hauntings are not associated with Berkeley Hundred and its attack in 1622, but rather the mansion itself and its occupation during the Civil War.

Since Berkeley was renovated in 1907, people have heard the sound of loud footsteps coming from the attic. When investigated, there would be no obvious cause for the sound. For the skeptic, this could be explained by the house settling or other natural phenomena. However, the other paranormal events experienced at Berkeley Plantation are not so easily debunked.

In the upstairs bedroom where William Harrison IV and his two daughters were fatally struck by lightning, there have been several sightings of a young woman holding a baby in the window. This is most often seen from the outside, but there have been occasions when people have seen her standing at the window while they were walking by the open door of the bedroom.

The sound of footsteps in the parlor has been heard. The footsteps are often accompanied by the apparition of a man that fits the description of William Harrison IV. Although most believe that it is his apparition, others speculate that the ghost of General McClellan is responsible. Although unrelated, the chandelier crystals have been known to move on their own and the door to a linen closet in the room open and closes by itself.

The ghosts of Union and Confederate soldiers have been seen near Berkeley Mansion. One Union soldier has been seen looking out over the nearby James River. Other soldiers have been seen standing near the front of the main entryway of the mansion. A Confederate soldier has been seen near the cellar where McClellan held prisoners for questioning.

Finally, there have been hundreds of sightings of an unidentified boy about ten years old standing near the edge of the Harrison family cemetery. There is sometimes a tall Union soldier standing beside him.

EDGEWOOD PLANTATION
Charles City

Edgewood Plantation was originally part of Berkeley Plantation until 1849 when Spencer Rowland purchased several hundred acres and founded his own plantation. Rowland, who moved to Charles City from New England a few years previously, purchased the property because he realized its income potential due to its proximity to the James River. A grist mill had been built by earlier owners of the property in 1725. Over a century later, Rowland saw that it was still in very good condition. Five years after purchasing his new plantation and grist mill, Rowland built a three-story Gothic Revival house at Edgewood in 1854.

Rowland put the grist mill to use, and plantation owners from miles around visited Edgewood to grind their corn into meal because many planters did not have grist mills on their property. Interestingly enough, during the Civil War both Confederate and Union troops took turns using the mill to grind their own corn meal.

During the Civil War, Confederate troops used the plantation house as a lookout and signal post to spy on approaching Union soldiers. General J.E.B. Stuart made a brief stop at Edgewood while en route to visit General Robert E. Lee in Richmond to inform him of the advancing power of the Union forces. While Stuart had coffee and refreshments inside, many of his Confederate soldiers waited patiently outside.

Over the years, Edgewood Plantation has served not only as a Civil War lookout but also as a post office, a nursing home, and a restaurant. In the 1970s, the Edgewood Plantation House was renovated into a comfortable and hospitable bed-and-breakfast.

At least three ghosts haunt Edgewood Plantation. Two of the three ghosts have been positively identified as people connected to the plantation, while the identity of the third ghost remains unknown at this time.

The most prominent ghost at Edgewood is that of Elizabeth "Lizzie" Rowland, the only sister of plantation owner Spencer Rowland. While living at Edgewood, Lizzie met and fell in love with Bernard Carter, the son of the owner of nearby Shirley Plantation. Bernard and Lizzie were inseparable and started to make wedding plans when the Civil War broke out. Feeling that it was his patriotic duty, Bernard volunteered to fight for the Confederacy. He asked Lizzie to wait for him and when he returned they would be married. Lizzie agreed and the two parted ways, never to see each other again.

After Bernard's departure, Lizzie spent hours looking out a second-floor window hoping to see her fiancé return from the war. One day while waiting for him, she carved her name into the wooden window-sill, which can be seen to this day. After months of waiting, Lizzie fell into a deep depression but never gave up hope that Bernard would one day return to her. She died at forty-seven years of age on February 6, 1870, still waiting in vain for his return. Upon her death, Lizzie was buried in the Westover Church graveyard a few miles from Edgewood Plantation.

Only a few months after her death, people who lived at Edgewood started to see Lizzie's ghost. Originally, the apparition of a woman in her mid-twenties to early thirties was only noticed near the windowsill where Lizzie had carved her name while waiting for her fiancé's return. Visitors have looked up to the second-floor window and have seen the apparition of a very sad, dark-haired woman looking down toward them. Eyewitnesses have also seen Lizzie's apparition from the inside as they reach the top of the stairs and look in the direction of the window. This story is very well documented in Marguerite Du Pont Lee's 1930 book, *Virginia Ghosts*.

After some time, Lizzie was witnessed in several parts of the house, including the kitchen and main stairway. People who have seen Lizzie's ghost have always said that she is very friendly and is most often seen on the first floor of the house.

In 1978, the plantation was purchased and converted into a very cozy bed-and-breakfast. In 2001, a guest who was a self-proclaimed sensitive visited Edgewood and requested a secluded area in order to ensure her privacy. The next morning, the woman complained to the bed-and-breakfast's owner that the room she stayed in was haunted by a young woman and demanded a room that did not have any ghosts, because they had a tendency to speak with her.

To accommodate her wishes, the guest was moved to the slave quarters where there had been no prior reports of hauntings. The next morning, the woman decided to check out because she had spent most of the night speaking with the ghost of a Confederate soldier named Aaron Young.

Word got out, and a few years later, Edgewood was featured on a fourth-season episode of *Ghost Hunters*. Although the ghost hunters found some ghostly activity associated with Lizzie, the epicenter of the activity took place in the slave quarters. Again, the name Aaron Young came up during the investigation. Historical records were searched and it was discovered there had been a Confederate soldier named Aaron Young III who belonged to Virginia's Twentieth Regiment, which passed near Edgewood Plantation. Although Young was identified as the ghost, it is uncertain why his ghost haunts the plantation, considering he moved west after the Civil War and died in Wirt County, West Virginia, in 1913.

A third ghost associated with Edgewood Plantation is that of an unidentified man who is only seen in a guest room known as Jeb's Room. Unlike Lizzie and Aaron, there has been no documentation found to help identify this man. He has been described as rather tall and slender. When his apparition is seen, the man is usually standing by the bed. When he is approached or after a few seconds, the ghost disappears.

FALL HILL PLANTATION
Fredericksburg

In February 1720, Francis Thornton acquired approximately 8,000 acres of property near Fredericksburg, and he built the first of two plantation houses on the property fifteen years later. The plantation was passed through four generations until it came into the ownership of Francis Thornton V, who in 1790 built a two-story brick Georgian mansion as a wedding gift to his wife, Sally Innes.

The property remained in the Thornton family until 1845, when Francis Thornton V died without a will naming someone to inherit Fall Hill. The plantation went up for sale and was bought by Dr. John Taylor, who kept the property in his name until 1870.

During the Civil War, the plantation house was in danger of being demolished by Confederate General Robert E. Lee when he and his troops were stationed in the Fredericksburg area. The property near the plantation house was close to the Rappahannock River, which gave

Lee a vantage point to observe the Union forces that were approaching the plantation. Lee considered burning the mansion to keep it from falling into Union hands, and the only reason that Lee did not destroy the house was that the Union troops he was spying on changed direction.

After the Civil War, Dr. Taylor returned to Fall Hill, where he repaired the mansion from damage caused by Confederate occupation. At this time, he also married a descendant of Francis Thornton V, which brought the property back into the Thornton family. Fall Hill remained in the Thornton family until 2003, when the last descendant passed away at 103 years of age.

For over 200 years, residents of and visitors to Fall Hill have experienced the ghost of a caretaker named Katina. Although stories of Katina's ghost were initially shared among family and close friends, one of the first documented accounts of paranormal phenomena at Fall Hill goes back to the 1920s, when a visitor wrote about her own encounter and shared it with her friends. Soon, Katina's story became widely known throughout the state.

Katina's ghost is described as an older, dark-complected woman with long, straight, graying hair. Unlike with some ghosts, those who have seen Katina usually feel a strong sense of peace and love. Sometimes, people who have seen Katina get the impression that she is either lost or looking for something. The sound of children laughing and playing can be heard in the nursery room and in the adjacent hallway from where Katina's ghost is usually seen.

Sometimes, Katina's ghost has been accompanied by a little boy about five years old. When he is seen with Katina, he is always holding her right hand. As with other apparitions, Katina's ghost will disappear if approached or confronted directly.

HAW BRANCH PLANTATION
Amelia

Haw Branch Plantation was founded in 1735 when Colonel Thomas Tabb purchased a tract of land outside of present-day Amelia, Virginia, for his wife, Rebecca. Over the next several years, Colonel Tabb and his wife expanded the property by several hundred acres. From 1745 to 1748, Tabb built a moderately sized Federal-style plantation house to live in while he oversaw the daily business of the plantation. By 1798, the property grew to over 2,700 acres. After Colonel Tubb's daughter Marianna inherited the property as a wedding gift when she married William Barksdale in 1815, the house was renovated once again. More of the surrounding property was purchased, and Tabb's daughter and her husband expanded their plantation to over 10,000 acres by the beginning of the Civil War.

After the Civil War ended, the plantation house lay vacant for several years. Most of the acreage of the plantation was sold to pay off a number of debts accrued by the Tabb family during the Civil War. Within a decade, Haw Branch Plantation dwindled from over 10,000 acres down to only 120 acres.

In recent years, Haw Branch has developed the reputation of being haunted, with ghosts ranging from farmhands to former residents.

The first ghost is that of a man carrying a gas lantern near where the plantation's barn stood. He is described as a tall, thin man with a pronounced limp. His apparition shows up randomly and appears to be simply making certain that the barn is secure. Similarly, the ghost of a female housekeeper or servant has been seen standing on the porch. As with the farmhand, her apparition is seen on occasion and does not appear to be malicious in any way.

A third ghost at Haw Branch Plantation appears to be located in the attic and the stairway leading to the attic. Over the years, several witnesses have heard the loud scream of a woman who sounds as if she is in extreme pain. The screaming is fairly predictable in that it only manifests once every six months. Most accounts report that the screams can be heard on or near May 23 and November 23 of each year. The screams always take place in the middle of the night, and when someone is brave enough to go to the attic to investigate, it is always empty.

Occasionally the screams are accompanied by the apparition of a young woman wearing either a nightgown or a long dress standing at the bottom of the stairway that leads to the attic. In the room adjacent to the attic stairs, people have noticed the smell of either roses or a rose-scented perfume just before the screaming takes place. It is believed that the ghost is of a girl who lived at the mansion shortly after it was built and that late one night, she fell down the attic stairs and died. Those who follow this train of thought believe that the anniversary of her death is either on May 23 or November 23, which would explain why her screams are only heard on those dates.

Kenmore Plantation
Fredericksburg

Kenmore is a 1,300-acre plantation, located near Fredericksburg, Virginia, that was originally owned by Colonel Fielding Lewis. Construction of the Georgian-style plantation house began in 1752 and was completed in early 1776. While the mansion was being constructed, Colonel Lewis, his wife, and their eleven children stayed on the property. The plantation stayed in the Lewis family from the early 1750s until it was sold out of the family because of financial difficulties in 1797.

An interesting bit of history associated with Kenmore Plantation is that Fielding Lewis's wife was Betty Washington Lewis, sister to first president of the United States, George Washington. As Lewis's plantation was not far from George Washington's own plantation, Mount Vernon, it was not uncommon to see him there on a regular basis to visit his sister.

Fielding Lewis grew and sold crops such as corn, tobacco, and wheat on the 1,300-acre plantation. Being a devout patriot, Lewis believed so much in the principles of the emerging American government that he invested most of his money into financing the Fredericksburg Arms Manufactory, which provided weapons and ammunition to colonists during the Revolutionary War. Lewis was promised by Virginia's government that he would be recognized and reimbursed for his generous contribution to the American cause. However, the money that Lewis invested was never repaid, which all but destroyed him financially. Lewis died at the age of fifty-six in December 1781. Some believed that he worried himself to an early grave because of his financial concerns.

After Lewis's death in 1781, his widow gained control of the plantation until her death sixteen years later. Still in considerable financial straits after Lewis's investment in the Fredericksburg Arms Manufactory, his sons sold the mansion and surrounding acreage in 1797.

The property went through a few owners until it was purchased in 1819 by Samuel Golden, who named the plantation Kenmore after an ancestral home in Scotland. After purchasing the property, Golden made several modifications to the mansion and lived there until the beginning of the Civil War.

The ghost of Fielding Lewis is believed to haunt the second-floor bedroom that he had converted into an office. In this room Lewis spent many sleepless nights trying to find a way to make enough money to ensure that he and his family would be financially secure. Sometimes, Lewis's ghost appears to be holding a piece of paper or parchment. Even if the apparition is not seen, the sound of heavy footsteps, described by some as pacing, can be heard from within this room, especially at night.

PINEY GROVE AT SOUTHALL'S PLANTATION
Holdcroft

In the late 1700s, Furneau Southall purchased approximately 300 acres outside of Holdcroft, Virginia. After founding the plantation, Southall acted as deputy sheriff of Charles City County. He also was one of the men responsible for administering the first official census of the area in 1790.

The plantation remained in the Southall family from 1790 until 1857, when Furneau's grandson, John Stubblefield, sold the property to Edmond Saunders. After purchasing Southall Plantation, Saunders opened a general store on the property and called it the Piney Grove Store, hence the name Piney Grove at Southall Plantation. Saunders's business was fortunate in that it was not greatly affected by the Civil War. Saunders kept fairly neutral during the war, which is likely one of the reasons that the Piney Grove Store remained in operation until 1915.

The property was sold two times from 1915 until the current owners renovated the plantation house and other buildings from 1984 to 1989. Today, the main plantation house is a bed-and-breakfast that offers tours and hosts local events throughout the year.

Compared with other plantations, such as the Myrtles Plantation in Louisiana, Piney Grove at Southall Plantation does not appear to have a remarkable history when it comes to the paranormal. However, there have been a few stories passed down through the years about a former clerk who is believed to haunt the store that was central to the plantation's success.

Thomas Fletcher Harwood, a clerk at the general store at Piney Grove from 1874 to 1915, is believed to haunt the store. During the Civil War, Thomas lost his leg because of cannon fire at the Battle of Malvern Hill on July 1, 1862. After surviving the amputation of most of his leg, a prosthetic leg was made for him by colleague and fellow veteran Jim Hanger. After being discharged from the Confederate army, Harwood returned to Piney Grove and became a clerk at the general store until his death in 1915.

Since Harwood's death, people have heard the distinct sound of footsteps on the front porch and inside the store. Sometimes the footsteps have been accompanied by a shadowy apparition. It is believed that the ghost is that of Mr. Harwood, based on the distinct sound of the footsteps. An encounter with Mr. Harwood's ghost so inspired one poet that she wrote a poem about not only his death, but also a family member's personal account of his encounter with his ghost.

ROSEWELL

Gloucester

After buying property to start a plantation in 1725, Mann Page built a 12,000-square-foot, three-story, Flemish bond brickwork mansion. Wanting his plantation mansion to be unique, Page hired and brought a renowned architect from England to ensure that the plantation house was built exactly to his specifications. When it was completed, Rosewell Mansion was one of the largest and most elaborate mansions built in Virginia at the time. Page imported building materials, trim work, paint, and many other supplies directly from England. The foundation walls were over three feet thick, which made it not only one of the most elaborate mansions in Virginia, but also one of the sturdiest.

Mann Page died shortly before his mansion was completed. Upon his death in 1730, his widow, Judith Carter Page, inherited the mansion and construction was suspended until Page's son, Mann Page Jr., inherited Rosewell. He followed his father's architectural style and the mansion was completed in 1738.

There is a great deal of historical significance associated with Rosewell Plantation. Thomas Jefferson was a good friend of the Page family and visited them whenever he could. It is believed that an early draft of the Declaration of Independence was written by Jefferson in a guest room at the mansion.

In 1837 Rosewell Plantation was sold to Thomas Booth. After removing and selling most of the imported materials used in the mansion's construction, he gave the mansion to his cousin, who sold it a few years later to Josiah Deans in 1853.

Unlike most plantations in Virginia, Rosewell remained unharmed during the Civil War. After the Civil War, Rosewell was abandoned and left to the elements for nearly fifty years. In 1916, Rosewell mansion burned to the ground, still abandoned at the time of the fire. Today, the mansion ruins are open to the public and can be toured.

There appear to be four separate hauntings associated with Rosewell Plantation, which include two women, two boys, and several unexplained sounds.

Although the mansion is no longer standing, the apparition of a young woman is seen near where the stairs to the front entrance once stood. She is always seen at dusk and only appears for a few seconds before disappearing.

In the same general vicinity as the young woman are the apparitions of two young boys seen standing near the front entrance where the phantom woman is encountered. Both boys are described as about twelve years old and wearing similar outfits. The boys appear to be holding lanterns in front of them, which was not uncommon during parties at plantations. Young boys held lanterns and helped guests enter and exit their carriages. Sometimes the sound of horse hooves can be heard in conjunction with the apparitions of the two boys.

A third apparition seen at Rosewell Plantation is of another young woman described as wearing a long red dress. Sometimes she is seen standing in front of the mansion ruins, but more frequently she is seen walking through the area where the Rosewell rose garden once stood.

In addition to these apparitions, there are also sounds that cannot be explained. Behind the plantation house ruins, muffled voices in hushed conversation have been heard. It has been suspected that these voices belong to the ghosts of slaves coming in from the fields.

REFERENCES

INTRODUCTION

"History of Trade, Plantations, Colonialism and Colonization in the 13 Colonies." Plantations. http://landofthebrave.info/plantations. htm.

ONE: HISTORY OF PLANTATIONS

Mitchell, Margaret. *Gone with the Wind*. New York: Macmillan, 1936.

TWO: ALABAMA

Cedarhurst Plantation

Williams, Yona. "Haunted Mansions in Alabama." Unexplainable. net. http://www.unexplainable.net/ghost-paranormal/haunted_ mansions_in_alabama.php.

Dr. John R Drish House/Drish Plantation

"Drish House." *Historic Tuscaloosa*. Tuscaloosa County Preservation Society. http://www.historictuscaloosa.org/index. php?page=drish-house.

"Haunted Places in Alabama." Tuscaloosa Paranormal Research Group. http://tuscaloosaparanormal.com/index.php?option=com_content&view=article&id=130&Itemid=97.

"Haunted Places Index—Alabama." The Shadowlands. http://www.theshadowlands.net/places/alabama.htm.

Stevenson, Tommy. "Drish House finally gets a chance to yield its secrets." *Tuscaloosa News.* October 13, 2008.

Windham, Kathryn Tucker and Margaret Gillis Figh. *13 Alabama Ghosts and Jeffrey.* Strode Publishers, 1969. 23–32.

Windham, Kathryn Tucker. *Jeffrey's Latest 13: More Alabama Ghosts.* Huntsville, Alabama: Strode Publishers, 1982. 21–32.

Forks of Cypress

"Forks of Cypress." Haunted Places. http://www.hauntedplaces.org/item/forks-of-cypress.

"Haunted Places Index—Alabama." The Shadowlands. http://www.theshadowlands.net/places/alabama.htm.

Gaineswood

"Demopolis-Gaineswood Plantation." "Haunted Places and Ghosts in Montgomery, Alabama" on HauntingsGuide.com. http://hauntingsguide.com/AlabamaHauntsMontgomeryArea.html.

"Gaineswood National Historic Landmark." "Encyclopedia of Alabama." Alabama Humanities Foundation. http://www.encyclopediaofalabama.org/face/Article.jsp?id=h-3020.

"Haunted Places in Alabama." Tuscaloosa Paranormal Research Group. http://tuscaloosaparanormal.com/index.php?option=com_content&view=article&id=130&Itemid=97.

"Real Haunted Stories of Real Haunted Places!" Haunted Places To Go! http://www.haunted-places-to-go.com.

"Haunted Places Index—Alabama." The Shadowlands. http://www.theshadowlands.net/places/alabama.htm.

Windham, Kathryn Tucker and Margaret Gillis Figh. *13 Alabama Ghosts and Jeffrey.* Strode Publishers, 1969. 55.

Kenworthy Hall / Carlisle-Martin House / Carlisle Hall

"Kenworthy Hall." National Register of Historic Places. http://pdf-host.focus.nps.gov/docs/NHLS/Text/90001318.pdf.

"Kenworthy Hall at Marion, AL (1858-1860)." Rural Southwest Alabama. http://www.ruralswalabama.org/attractions/kenworthy-hall-1858-1860.

Smithers, Tashery. Telephone interview. January 15, 2014.

Rocky Hill Castle / Rocky Hill

Hauck, Dennis William. *Haunted Places: The National Directory: Ghostly Abodes, Sacred Sites, UFO Landings and Other Supernatural Locations.* Penguin, 1996. 225.

Windham, Kathryn Tucker and Margaret Gillis Figh. *13 Alabama Ghosts and Jeffrey.* Strode Publishers, 1969. 13–21.

Spring Villa

"Arthur Yonge." *Genealogy Magazine.* http://www.genealogymagazine.com/arthuryonge.html.

B. B. Paddock. *History and Biographical Record of North and West Texas.* Vol. II. Chicago: Lewis Publishing Co., 1906. 411-413.

"Haunted Places and Ghosts in Montgomery, Alabama" on HauntingsGuide.com. http://hauntingsguide.com/AlabamaHauntsMontgomeryArea.html.

"Haunted Places in Alabama." Tuscaloosa Paranormal Research Group. http://tuscaloosaparanormal.com/index.php?option=com_content&view=article&id=130&Itemid=97.

"Haunted Places Index—Alabama." The Shadowlands. http://www.theshadowlands.net/places/alabama.htm.

"National Register Information System." *National Register of Historic Places.* National Park Service. March 13, 2009.

"Spring Villa." City of Opelika. http://www.opelika.org/Default. asp?ID=152.

Sturdivant Mansion / Watts-Parkman-Gillman Home

Hammond, Ralph. *Antebellum Mansions of Alabama*. New York: Architectural Book Publishers, 1951. 140–143.

"Haunted Places in Alabama." Tuscaloosa Paranormal Research Group. http://tuscaloosaparanormal.com/index.php?option=com_content&view=article&id=130&Itemid=97.

Hendrix, Kim. "The Ghost That Lives In Sturdivant Hall In Selma." WSFA.com. http://www.wsfa.com/story/3689284/the-ghost-that-lives-in-sturdivant-hall-in-selma.

"Haunted Places Index—Alabama." The Shadowlands. http://www.theshadowlands.net/places/alabama.htm.

Windham, Kathryn Tucker and Margaret Gillis Figh. *13 Alabama Ghosts and Jeffrey*. Huntsville, Alabama: Strode Publishers, 1969.

Sweetwater Plantation

"Southern Discomfort." *Paranormal State*. A&E. April 25, 2011.

"John Brahan." Huntsville History Collection. April 2014. http://huntsvillehistorycollection.org/hh/index.php?title=Person:John_Brahan.

Delinski, Bernie. "Sweetwater Mansion Site of Paranormal Activity Hunters." *Times Daily* (Florence, AL). October 30, 2011. http://www.timesdaily.com/archives/article_f2262411-b43c-5bab-968f-40c953f0496d.html.

"Haunted Places Index—Alabama." The Shadowlands. http://www.theshadowlands.net/places/alabama.htm.

Three: Georgia
Antebellum Plantation

"Antebellum Plantation." Spook Hunters. http://www.spookhunters.com/spookhunt/stonemountain/hunt.php.

"Stone Mountain Park's Antebellum Plantation." Strange USA. http://www.strangeusa.com/Viewlocation.aspx?id=2607#sthash. sOnshhPa.dpbs.

"The Boy in Thornton House." Ghostvillage.com. http://www. ghostvillage.com/encounters/2009/06192009.shtml.

"The Oldest House in Georgia." *Ghost Hunters.* Syfy Network. October 27, 2010. http://www.syfy.com/ghosthunters/episodes/season/s06/episode/e620/the_oldest_house_in_georgia.

Barnsley Gardens/Adair House

"Barnsley Gardens." *Barnsley Resort.* Rise Up Paranormal. http://www.riseupparanormal.com/paranormal-world/locations/Barnsley_Gardens.htm.

"Barnsley Gardens." Roadside Georgia. http://roadsidegeorgia.com/site/barnsley.html.

"Barnsley Gardens Resort." Haunt Spot: Ghost Stories, Ghost Photos, and Real Hauntings. http://www.hauntspot.com/haunt/usa/georgia/barnsley-gardens-resort.shtml.

"Haunted Places in Georgia." The Shadowlands. http://www.the-shadowlands.net/places/georgia.htm.

"History." Barnsley Resort. http://www.barnsleyresort.com/history.aspx.

Bonaventure Cemetery

Brown, Russell K. "Josiah Tattnall (ca. 1764-1803)." *New Georgia Encyclopedia.* July 16, 2006. http://www.georgiaencyclopedia.org/articles/government-politics/josiah-tattnall-ca-1764-1803.

Burgoyne, Mindie. "Bonaventure Cemetery—Ghosts, Gardens and Art on the Wilmington River." *Who Cares What I Think?* http://www.marylandwriter.net/2011/03/bonaventure-cemetery-savannahs.html.

"History." Bonaventure Historical Society. http://www.bonaventurehistorical.org/bonaventure/history.

"Josiah Tattnall of Bonaventure." Georgia Pioneers. http://www.
georgiapioneers.com/goldenisles/tattnall.html.

Pierce, Hudson. "Bonaventure Plantation and Cemetery." HubPages.
http://hudsonpierce.hubpages.com/hub/httphudsonpiercehub-
pagescom.

"The Ghosts of Savannah's Bonaventure Cemetery." Ghosts and
Ghouls. http://ghostsnghouls.com/2012/11/25/haunted-bonaven-
ture-cemetery.

Bulloch Hall

Bumsted, Phoebe. "Ghostly Haunts of Historic Roswell." North-
fulton.com. October 24, 2012. http://www.northfulton.com/
Articles-TOP-STORIES-c-2012-10-24-195656.114126-sub-Ghostly-
haunts-of-Historic-Roswell.html#123.

"Family History." Bulloch Hall. http://www.bullochhall.org/family-
history.html.

"Ghostly Sounds—Cheetham Hill and Bulloch Hall." Haunted
Georgia. December 2008. http://hauntedgeorgia.wordpress.com/
tag/bulloch-hall/.

"The Ghosts of Bulloch Hall." *The Beacon Newspaper*. March 27, 2010.
http://www.beaconcastmedia.com/lifestyle/The-Ghosts-of-Bull-
och-Hall-1825.

Early Hill Plantation

"Early Hill Bed and Breakfast." Strange USA. http://www.strange-
usa.com/Viewlocation.aspx?id=2491&desc=%20Early%20
Hill%20Bed%20and%20Breakfast%20%20Greensboro%20%20
Ga#sthash.3NM6BGCW.dpbs.

"Haunted Places in Georgia." The Shadowlands. http://www.the-
shadowlands.net/places/georgia.htm.

"List of National Historic Landmarks by State." *National Historic
Landmarks Survey*. http://web.archive.org/web/20070609212946/
http://www.cr.nps.gov/nhl/designations/Lists/LIST07.pdf.

Ezekiel Harris House

"1797 Ezekiel Harris House." Augusta Museum of History. http://www.augustamuseum.org/HarrisHouse.

"Ezekiel Harris House." http://www.inusa.com/tour/ga/augusta/harris.htm.

"Harrisburg-West End and Woodlawn Historic District." Historic Augusta, Incorporated. http://www.historicaugusta.org/preservation/historic-districts/harrisburg-west-end-and-woodlawn.

Gaither Plantation

City of Covington. http://www.cityofcovington.org/Pages/home.aspx.

"Gaither Plantation." *Haunted Places.* http://www.hauntedplaces.org/item/gaither-plantation.

Lockerly Plantation

"History." *Lockerly Arboretum.* http://www.lockerly.org/history.php.

"Lockerly Spirits are Quiet This Year." *Union Recorder* (Midgeville, GA). October 30, 2006. http://www.unionrecorder.com/feature/x155357961/Lockerly-spirits-are-quiet-this-year.

Stately Oaks Plantation

"Stately Oaks." Historical Jonesboro. http://www.historicaljonesboro.org.

"The Haunting of Stately Oaks Plantation." YouTube. October 27, 2010. http://www.youtube.com/watch?v=pe6FxZ8jiho.

FOUR: LOUISIANA

Chretien Point Plantation

"Chretien Point Plantation." Southern Spirit Guide: "Haunted Louisiana." http://southernspiritguide.blogspot.com/2011/01/haunted-louisiana.html.

"The Battle of Buzzard's Prairie, Louisiana." The South's Defender. October 26, 2013. http://thesouthsdefender.blogspot.com/2013/10/150-years-ago-battle-of-buzzards.html.

"The Mistress of Chretien Point." Chretienpoint.com. http://www.chretienpoint.com/the-mistress-of-chretien-point.

Destrehan Plantation

"Destrehan Manor Museum." HauntedHouses.com. http://www.hauntedhouses.com/states/la/destrehan_manor.htm.

"Destrehan Plantation History." Destrehan Plantation. http://www.destrehanplantation.org/history.html.

Powell, Lewis IV. "Haunted Plantations of Louisiana's River Road, Part I." Southern Spirit Guide. 2011. http://southernspiritguide.blogspot.com/2010/09/haunted-plantations-of-louisianas-river.html.

"Haunted Places Index—Louisiana." The Shadowlands. http://www.theshadowlands.net/places/louisiana.htm.

Taylor, Troy. "Destrehan Manor." Prairie Ghosts. http://www.prairieghosts.com/destrehan.html.

The Houmas/Burnside Plantation

"Houmas House Ghosts." Houmas House Plantation and Gardens. http://www.houmashouse.com/ghosts.htm.

"The Houmas." National Park Service. http://www.nps.gov/nr/travel/louisiana/hou.htm.

LeBeau Plantation

"LeBeau Plantation House." Roadtrippers. https://roadtrippers.com/places/LeBeau-plantation-house-arabi/51a808954203c35137002462.

Wells, Carlie K. "Seven Suspects in LeBeau Plantation Fire Were Looking for Ghosts, Sheriff Says." NOLA.com. November 22, 2013. http://www.nola.com/crime/index.ssf/2013/11/seven_people_in_custody_for_le.html.

Loyd Hall Plantation

"Loyd Hall Plantation Bed & Breakfast in Cheneyville Louisiana Available for Weddings, Events and Tour Groups." Loyd Hall Plantation. http://www.loydhall.com.

"Haunted Places Index—Louisiana." The Shadowlands. http://www.theshadowlands.net/places/louisiana.htm.

Magnolia Plantation

"Magnolia Plantation History." National Park Service. http://www.nps.gov/cari/historyculture/magnolia-plantation-history.htm.

"Magnolia Plantation." Travel Channel. http://www.travelchannel.com/tv-shows/ghost-adventures/articles/magnolia-plantation-haunted-history.

"National Register Information System." *National Register of Historic Places.* National Park Service. March 13, 2009.

Myrtles Plantation

"America's Most Haunted: Myrtles Plantation." Prairieghosts.com. 2013. http://www.prairieghosts.com/myrtles.html.

Kermeen, Frances. *The Myrtles Plantation: The True Story of America's Most Haunted House.* New York: Warner, 2005.

"Haunted Places Index—Louisiana." The Shadowlands. http://www.theshadowlands.net/places/louisiana.htm.

"The Myrtles Plantation." The Myrtles Plantation. http://www.myrtlesplantation.com.

Oak Alley Plantation/Bon Sejour

Cumerlato, Daniel. "Oak Alley Plantation." Ghost Walks and Dark History Tours. http://www.ghostwalks.com/oakalleyplantation-article.htm.

Powell, Lewis IV. "Haunted Plantations of Louisiana's River Road, Part I." Southern Spirit Guide. http://southernspiritguide.

blogspot.com/2010/09/haunted-plantations-of-louisianas-river.
html.

"Haunted Places Index—Louisiana." The Shadowlands. http://
www.theshadowlands.net/places/louisiana.htm.

"The Shadows of Oak Alley." Oak Alley Plantation. http://www
.oakalleyplantation.com/learn-explore/ghost-tales.

San Francisco Plantation

"Hauntings and Ghostly Sightings." New Orleans Plantation Country. http://www.neworleansplantationcountry.com/about/haunt-
ings.

"San Francisco Plantation." San Francisco Plantation. http://www
.sanfranciscoplantation.orghistory.asp.

Shadows-on-the-Teche

Hall, Justin. "Haunting Storytelling." *The Daily Iberian* (New Iberia,
LA). October 24, 2010. http://www.iberianet.com/news/haunt-
ing-storytelling/article_cd1a263b-cec6-5161-a7d5-2ab51c3026f9.
html.

"The Shadows." The Shadows-On-The-Teche. http://shadowson-
theteche.org.

Woodland Plantation

Cumerlato, Daniel. "Woodland Plantation." Ghost Walks and Dark
History Tours. http://www.ghostwalks.com/woodlandplanta-
tion-article.htm.

"EVPs at Woodland Plantation." Cajun Ghost Hunter. http://cajung-
hosthunter.com/EVPs_Woodland_Plantation.html.

"Woodland Plantation." Paranormal Stories. http://paranormalsto-
ries.blogspot.com/2009/06/woodland-plantation.html.

"Woodland Plantation History." Woodland Plantation and Spirits
Hall. http://www.woodlandplantation.com/history.htm.

FIVE: MISSISSIPPI

Anchuca Plantation

"Anchuca Mansion, Vicksburg, MS." Anchuca Mansion Bed and Breakfast. http://www.anchucamansion.com.

Hauck, Dennis William. *Haunted Places: The National Directory: A Guidebook to Ghostly Abodes, Sacred Sites, UFO Landings, and Other Supernatural Locations.* New York: Penguin, 1996.

"Mary Chastain Archer (1838–1900)." Find A Grave Memorial. http://www.findagrave.com/cgi-bin/fg.cgi?page=gr&GRid=53032789.

"Mississippi Haunted Houses: Vicksburg Hauntings, Anchuca Mansion." Hauntedhouses.com. http://www.hauntedhouses.com/states/ms/anchuca.htm.

"Real Mississippi Hauntings-Anchuca Mansion." Squidoo. http://www.squidoo.com/HauntMississippi.

"The Haunting of Anchuca Mansion." True Hauntings of America: Mississippi. October 25, 2007. http://hauntsofamerica.blogspot.com/search/label/Mississippi.

Beauvoir

Discussion on Beauvoir. Telephone interview with Charles L. Sullivan. January 21, 2014.

Dickinson, Nancy M. "The History and Hauntings of Beauvoir." *BlogTalkRadio.* October 16, 2010. http://www.blogtalkradio.com/nancy-marine-dickinson/2010/10/16/experience-the-history-and-hauntings-of-beauvoir-biloxi-ms.

"History of Beauvoir." Beauvoir—The Jefferson Davis Home and Presidential Library. http://www.beauvoir.org/History_of_Beauvoir.html.

Cedar Grove

"Real Mississippi Hauntings-Cedar Grove." Squidoo. http://www
.squidoo.com/HauntMississippi.

"Vicksburg Mississippi Bed and Breakfast." Cedar Grove Inn. http://
www.cedargroveinn.com/index.php.

Lenoir Plantation House

"Mississippi's Lenoir Plantation." Nighthawk Publications. http://
www.nighthawkpublications.com/journal/2009/51/journal_1.
htm.

Longwood/Nutt's Folly

"Dr. Nutt of Longwood." Adams County, MS Genealogical and
Historical Research. http://www.natchezbelle.org/adams-ind/
folklore.htm#nutt.

"The History of Longwood Plantation." Natchez Ghosts, Natchez Area Paranormal Society. http://natchezghosts.blogspot.
com/2011/09/history-of-longwood-plantation-this.html.

Merrehope Mansion

Jacob, Jennifer. "Merrehope: Meridian's Haunted Mansion." *The Meridian Star* (Meridian, MS). October 28, 2007. http://meridianstar.
com/local/x681093071/Merrehope-Meridian-s-Haunted-Mansion.

"Merrehope." Merrehope.com. http://www.merrehope.com/his-
tory.html.

Monmouth

"Monmouth: Historical Overview." Monmouth Historic Inn. http://
www.monmouthhistoricinn.com/historical-overview.html.

"Monmouth Plantation, Natchez, Mississippi." Haunted Rooms:
Mississippi. http://www.hauntedrooms.com/monmouth-planta-
tion-natchez-mississippi.

"Monmouth Plantation." Hauntedhouses.com. http://www.haunt-edhouses.com/states/ms/monmouth.htm.

"Real Mississippi Hauntings-Monmouth." Squidoo. http://www.squidoo.com/HauntMississippi.

Waverly Plantation

"Five Antebellum Mansions." Columbus Hauntings, Antebellum Mansions. Hauntedhouses.com. http://www.hauntedhouses.com/states/ms/antebellum_mansions.htm.

"Haunted Mansion in Mississippi." Waverly Mansion & Gardens—West Point, Mississippi. http://www.exploresouthernhistory.com/waverly.html.

"Real Mississippi Hauntings—Waverly Plantation." Squidoo. http://www.squidoo.com/HauntMississippi.

Windsor Ruins

Murdock, Carol. "Did You See That?... The Ghost of Windsor." The Writers Porch. http://thewritersporch.blogspot.com/2009/01/did-you-see-that-ghost-of-windsor.html.

"Windsor Plantation: The Stately Columns Are All That Remain..." National Park Service. http://www.nps.gov/vick/forteachers/upload/Windsor-2.pdf.

"Windsor Ruins." *Examiner.com.* October 2, 2012. http://www.examiner.com/article/windsor-ruins.

SIX: NORTH CAROLINA

Bellamy Mansion

"Bellamy Mansion Ghosts." Port City Paranormal Team. http://www.portcityparanormal.com/BellamyMansion.html.

"Bellamy Mansion Museum." Bellamy Mansion Museum. http://www.bellamymansion.org.

"North Carolina Legends: The Bellamy Mansion." *The Sanford Family Misfit.* http://www.sanfordfamilymisfit.com/north-carolina-legends-the-bellamy-mansion.

Foscue Plantation

"Foscue Plantation History." Foscue Plantation. http://www.foscueplantation.com/.

"North Carolina Hauntings." Might Be Haunted-com. http%3A%2F%2Fwww.mightbehaunted.com%2FNORTH%2520CAROLINA.html.

"Pollocksville-Foscue Plantation." Forgotten USA. http://forgottenusa.com/haunts/NC/8530/Foscue%2520Plantation.

"Haunted Places Index—North Carolina." The Shadowlands. http://www.theshadowlands.net/places/northcarolina.htm.

"The Haunting of Foscue Plantation." North Carolina Hauntings. http://www.hauntin.gs/Foscue-Plantation_Pollocksville_North-Carolina_United-States_7857.

Grimesland Plantation

"The Grimes Plantation." Town of Grimesland, North Carolina RSS. http://grimesland.org/community/sites-to-see/grimes-plantation.

"The Haunting of Grimesland Plantation." Haunted Places in Grimesland, NC (North Carolina). http://www.hauntin.gs/Grimesland-Plantation_Grimesland_North-Carolina_United-States_9613.

Mordecai Plantation

"Mordecai Historic Park." Historical Resources and Museum Program. http://www.raleighnc.gov/mordecai.

"Mordecai House and USS North Carolina." *Ghost Hunters.* Syfy Network. August 17, 2005.

"Mordecai House." Raleigh: A Capital City. http://www.nps.gov/nr/travel/raleigh/mor.htm.

Smith-McDowell House

"If These Walls Could Talk: A History of the Smith-McDowell House." Smith-McDowell House Museum. The Western North Carolina Historical Association. http://www.wnchistory.org/people.html.

"Local Asheville Ghost Stories." Ghost Stories of Asheville, NC. Asheville Paranormal Society. http://www.ashevilleparanormal-society.com/ghoststories.html.

Stagville Plantation

"Haunted NC Historic Stagville Plantation." http://www.ncgypsy.com/haunted-nc-stagville-plantation.html.

"Haunted Stagville." Hauntedstories.net. http://hauntedstories.net/haunted-house/north-carolina/haunted-stagville.

"Historic Stagville." Haunted North Carolina. http://www.haunt-ednc.com/investigations/public-sites/historic-stagville.html.

"Stagville History." Stagville State Historic Site. http://www.stagville.org/history.

SEVEN: SOUTH CAROLINA
Boone Hall Plantation

Boone Hall Plantation. http://boonehallplantation.com.

Brick House Ruins

"Brick House Ruins, Charleston County (Edisto Island)." South Carolina Department of Archives and History. http://www.nationalregister.sc.gov/charleston/S10817710013/index.htm.

"Edisto Ghost Tales." Edisto Island, South Carolina. http://blog.edistoisland.com/edisto-ghost-tales.

"Haunted South Carolina." Southern Spirit Guide. February 24, 2011. http://southernspiritguide.blogspot.com/2011/02/haunted-south-carolina.html.

Spencer, Charles. *Edisto Island, 1663 to 1860: Wild Eden to Cotton Aristocracy*. Charleston: History, 2008.

Cool Springs

Battle, Margaret. "Cool Spring Plantation: One of Finest Edgecombe Antebellum Homes Burned to Ground in 1889." *The Rocky Mount Telegram*. April 23, 1967. http://www.thebattlebook.com/Cool-SpringPlantation.pdf.

Biles, DeDe. "Spooky South Carolina: Spirits Come Alive This Halloween." *Aiken Standard* (Aiken, SC). October 27, 2013. http://www.aikenstandard.com/article/20131027/AIK0401/131029524/1031/AIK04/spooky-south-carolina-spirits-come-alive-this-halloween.

"Cool Springs, Kershaw County." South Carolina Department of Archives and History. http://www.nationalregister.sc.gov/kershaw/S10817728013.

"The Party Ghost of Cool Springs Plantation." Hauntedstories.net. http://hauntedstories.net/haunted-houses/north-carolina/party-ghost-cool-springs-plantation.

Hampton Plantation/Hampton Plantation State Historic Site

"Civil War Gold And Other Lost Treasures." Rense.com. http://rense.com/general33/civil.htm.

Georgetown Times. October 27, 2010. http://www.gtowntimes.com/local/Ghosts--spirits-wander-Georgetown-County2010-10-27T08-57-25.

"Hampton Plantation." South Carolina Plantations. http://south-carolina-plantations.com/charleston/hampton.html.

"Hampton Plantation EVP Recording." *Angels & Ghosts*. http://www.angelsghosts.com/hampton_plantation_evp_recording.html.

"John Henry Rutledge." Find a Grave. April 22, 2006. http://www
.findagrave.com/cgi-bin/fg.cgi?page=gr&GRid=14023965.

South Carolina State Parks. http://www.southcarolinaparks.com.

Hermitage Plantation

"Haunted Locations in and around the Grand Strand and Pee Dee."
Haunted Halloween. http://static.mgnetwork.com/scp/media_
path/generic_page_gfx/halloween/haunted_places.html.

Ross, L. Woodrow. "Ghosts of South Carolina: Two Stories of Lost
Love and Tragic Death." *Independent Mail*, (Anderson, SC). May
21, 2011. http://www.independentmail.com/news/2011/may/21/
ghosts-south-carolina-two-stories-lost-love-and-tr.

Litchfield Plantation

Holland, Libba. "Paranormal Investigation: Pawleys Island Plantation History Sparks Ghost Stories among Visitors." *WBTW News*,
(Myrtle Beach, SC). June 27, 2013. http://www.wbtw.com/sto-
ry/22705382/paranormal-investigation-pawleys-island-plantation-
history-sparks-ghost-stories-among-visitors.

"Litchfield Plantation Ghost." Litchfield Plantation. http://litchfield-
plantation.net/history.

"Litchfield Plantation History." Litchfield Plantation. http://litch-
fieldplantation.net/litchfield-plantation-ghost.

"The Ghost of Litchfield Plantation." Hauntedstories.net. http://
hauntedstories.net/haunted-houses/south-carolina/ghost-litch-
field-plantation.

Magnolia Plantation and Gardens

"Ghost Hunters Season 8: Episode 18 Recap." *Reality Wanted*, October 10, 2012.

"Ghost Hunters: Magnolia Plantation Offers Plenty Of Paranormal." *Huffington Post*. October 11, 2012. http://www.huffingtonpost.com/2012/10/11/ghost-hunters-magnolia-plantation-video_n_1956846.html.

Magnolia Plantation and Gardens. http://www.magnoliaplantation.com.

The Oaks

Cote, Richard N. "Theodosia Burr Alston: Portrait of a Prodigy." Corinthian Books. http://www.bookdoctor.com/corinthian/cote/theodosia.html.

Stoney-Baynard Plantation/Baynard Ruins/ Braddock's Point Plantation

"Haunted Places in South Carolina." The Shadowlands. http://www.theshadowlands.net/places/southcarolina.htm.

Wooster, Lymann. "The Stoneys, the Baynards, and Their Mansion." Heritage Library Foundation. http://www.heritagelib.org/articles/the-stoneys-the-baynards-and-their-mansion.

Wedgefield Plantation

"Headless Apparition Haunts Wedgefield Plantation." *Most Haunted Places in America*. June 21, 2010. http://www.ghosteyes.com/british-dragoon-wedgefield-plantation.

King, Chris. "Five Things You Need To Know About Wedgefield Plantation." Myrtle Beach Golf Holiday. March 01, 2012. http://myrtlebeachgolf.golfholiday.com/blog/myrtle-beach-golf-news/five-things-you-need-to-know-about-wedgefield-plantation.

"Wedgefield Plantation—Georgetown—Georgetown County." South Carolina Plantations. http://south-carolina-plantations.com/georgetown/wedgefield-black-river.html.

EIGHT: VIRGINIA

Abijah Thomas House / Octagonal House

Bahr, Jeff, Troy Taylor, Loren Coleman, Mark Moran, and Mark Sceurman. *Weird Virginia: Your Travel Guide to Virginia's Local Legends and Best Kept Secrets.* New York: Sterling, 2007.

"Haunted Places Index—Virginia." The Shadowlands. http://www .theshadowlands.net/places/virginia.htm.

Appomattox Manor

"Appomattox Manor." James Rivers Plantations. http://www.nps. gov/nr/travel/jamesriver/app.htm.

"Haunted Places Index—Virginia." The Shadowlands. http://www .theshadowlands.net/places/virginia.htm.

Avenel House / William M. Burwell House

Marin, Patricia. "Haunted Avenel in Bedford, VA, Proves Active for Ghostec Paranormal Group." *Examiner.com.* May 1, 2011. http:// www.examiner.com/article/haunted-avenel-bedford-va-proves- active-for-ghostec-paranormal-group.

Belle Grove Plantation

"Belle Grove History." Belle Grove Plantation. http://www.belle- grove.org.

"Haunted Places Index—Virginia." The Shadowlands. http://www .theshadowlands.net/places/virginia.htm.

"The Gruesome Tale of Belle Grove Plantation." Ghost Place. Sep- tember 27, 2004. http://www.ghostplace.com/threads/the-grue- some-tale-of-belle-grove-plantation.2282.

Berkeley Plantation

"Berkeley Plantation History." Berkeley Plantation. www.berkeley- plantation.com.

"Five Haunted Virginia Plantations." The Edge of Reality. http://
theedgeofreality.proboards.com/thread/2332.

"The Restless Spirits at Berkeley Plantation." The Paranormal
File. October 21, 2012. http://theparanormalfile.wordpress.
com/2012/10/21/the-restless-spirits-at-berkeley-plantation.

Fall Hill Plantation

"Fall Hill Plantation—Fredericksburg, VA." The Haunted Com-
monwealth. November 28, 2010. http://hauntedva.blogspot.
com/2010/11/case-file-fall-hill-plantation.html.

"Nanny of Fall Hill." *Fredericksburg.com*. October 26, 2002. http://
www.fredericksburg.com/News/FLS/2002/102002/10262002/76
2610.

"Haunted Places Index—Virginia." The Shadowlands. http://www
.theshadowlands.net/places/virginia.htm.

Haw Branch Plantation

"Most Haunted Places in America: Haw Branch Plantation." *Ghost
Eyes RSS*. May 18, 2009. http://www.ghosteyes.com/haw-branch-
plantation-haunting.

"Haunted Places Index—Virginia." The Shadowlands. http://www
.theshadowlands.net/places/virginia.htm.

"The Haw Branch Hauntings." Virginia Ghosts. http://virginiag-
hosts.com/haw_branch.php.

Kenmore Plantation

"Haunting Tours of Historic Plantations, Sites." *Richmond Times
Dispatch*. October 23, 2009. http://www.timesdispatch.com/
entertainment-life/haunting-tours-of-historic-plantations-sites/
article_8f40a148-a205-59b1-8868-fe524881038f.html.

Historic Kenmore Plantation. http://www.kenmore.org.

Piney Grove at Southall's Plantation

"Landmark History." Piney Grove at Southall's Plantation. http://www.pineygrove.com/landmarkhistory.html.

Rosewell

"Historic Rosewell Remains Touch Gloucester Residents." *Daily Press* (Hampton Roads, VA). March 20, 1991. http://articles.daily-press.com/1991-03-20/news/9103200104_1_bricks-ruins-mansion.

Kinney, Pamela. "Supernatural Friday: Ghostly Stories of Rosewell Plantation in Gloucester, Virginia." September 9, 2011. http://pamelakkinney.blogspot.com/2011/09/ghostly-stroies-of-rosewell-plantation.html.

Lee, Marguerite DuPont. *Virginia Ghosts*. Rev ed. Berryville, VA: Virginia Book Company, 1966.

Melvin, Frank S. *National Register of Historic Place Nomination Form for Bacon's Castle*. Listed October 15, 1966.

Powell, Lewis IV. Southern Spirit Guide: Haunted Virginia. March 10, 2011. http://southernspiritguide.blogspot.com/2011/03/haunted-virginia.html.

"Haunted Places Index—Virginia." The Shadowlands. http://www.theshadowlands.net/places/virginia.htm.

Waterman, Thomas Tileston. *The Mansions of Virginia, 1706-1776*. Chapel Hill: University of North Carolina Press, 1946.

Kinney, Pamela K. *Virginia's Haunted Historic Triangle: Williamsburg, Yorktown, Jamestown, and Other Haunted Locations*. Atglen, PA: Schiffer Publishing, Ltd.

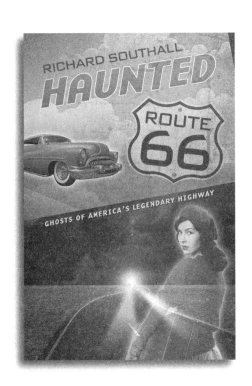

Haunted Route 66
Ghosts of America's Legendary Highway
RICHARD SOUTHALL

Pack the bags, hop in the car, and head west on a haunted journey of spine-tingling history and paranormal activity along legendary Route 66! This travel companion brings you from Chicago, Illinois, to Santa Monica, California, investigating over one hundred ghostly hot spots filled with fascinating facts and lingering spirits.

From amateur and professional ghost hunters to nostalgic fans, everyone can take their own haunted adventure on Route 66. Discover the famous highway through historic locations and gripping ghost stories about Al Capone and the gang wars of Chicago, Charlie Chaplin and the Venice Beach Boardwalk in Los Angeles, and many more. This one-of-a-kind collection, with chapters organized by state, paves the way for your grand tour.

978-0-7387-2636-6, 240 pp., 6 x 9   **$15.99**

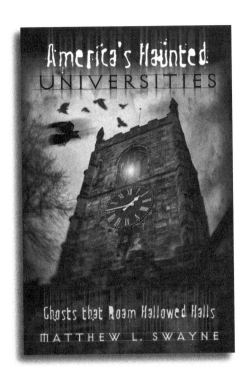

America's Haunted Universities
Ghosts that Roam Hallowed Halls
Matthew L. Swayne

America's Haunted Universities examines some of the most haunted locales in the country—U.S. university campuses. From haunted libraries to doomed dorms, journalist Matthew L. Swayne has scoured universities across the country to bring readers the most comprehensive look available at ghost encounters at these bastions of higher education. This guide explores the strangest and most enduring stories with first-hand accounts, historical analysis, and a re-telling of classic legends.

Readers will find stories about long-dead college faculty who still appear in a spectral sense on American campuses, coeds who met untimely ends, a haunted elevator, the carnivorous Penguin man, the ghostess with the mostess, and a poltergeist named "Monkey Boy," as well as many other chilling and bizarre entities and encounters.

978-0-7387-3080-6, 240 pp., 6 x 9   **$15.99**

GHOSTLY TALES OF MUSICAL LEGENDS

HAUNTED
ROCK &
ROLL

MATTHEW L. SWAYNE

Haunted Rock & Roll
Ghostly Tales of Musical Legends
Matthew L. Swayne

From rock and roll's pioneers to its contemporary rebels, explore how the greatest names live on after death—in unexpected and frightening ways. Combining two of America's great passions, celebrities and the paranormal, *Haunted Rock & Roll* covers rock's entire supernatural history.

Explore rock and roll's most iconic idols, haunted locations, and infamous legends through evidence and testimonials from renowned ghost hunters and researchers. Discover thrilling stories of Michael Jackson, Jim Morrison, Led Zeppelin, the Beatles, Amy Winehouse, and many more stars seen haunting their favorite bars, clubs, and homes. From the early days through the present pop music era, rockers have followed the same motto: Live fast, die young, and leave a restless spirit.

978-0-7387-3923-6, 288 pp., 5³⁄₁₆ x 8   **$15.99**

To order, call 1-877-NEW-WRLD
Prices subject to change without notice
Order at Llewellyn.com 24 hours a day, 7 days a week!

The Ghost Hunter's Field Guide
Over 1000 Haunted Places You Can Experience
RICH NEWMAN

Ghost hunting isn't just on television. More and more paranormal investigation groups are popping up across the nation. To get in on the action, you need to know where to go.

The Ghost Hunter's Field Guide features over 1,000 haunted places around the country in all fifty states. Visit battlefields, theaters, saloons, hotels, museums, resorts, parks, and other sites teeming with ghostly activity. Each location—haunted by the spirits of murderers, Civil War soldiers, plantation slaves, and others—is absolutely safe and accessible.

This indispensable reference guide features over 100 photos and offers valuable information for each location, including the tales behind the haunting and the kind of paranormal phenomena commonly experienced there: apparitions, shadow shapes, phantom aromas, telekinetic activity, and more.

978-0-7387-2088-3, 432 pp., 6 x 9   **$17.95**

MARK SPENCER

a

h a u n t e d

l o v e s t o r y

The Ghosts of the Allen House

A Haunted Love Story
The Ghosts of the Allen House
MARK SPENCER

A Haunted Love Story is two tales in one: a modern family's attempt to embrace their strange, spirit-inhabited home and a vintage love affair kept secret for six decades.

When Mark Spencer bought the beautiful old Allen House in Monticello, Arkansas, he knew that it was famously haunted. According to ghost lore, the troubled spirit of Ladell Allen, who mysteriously committed suicide in the master bedroom in 1948, still roamed the historic mansion. Yet Mark remained skeptical—until he and his family began witnessing faceless phantoms, a doppelganger spirit, and other paranormal phenomena. Ensuing ghost investigations offered convincing evidence that six spirits, including Ladell, inhabited their home. But the most shocking event occured the day Mark followed a strange urge to explore the attic and found, crammed under a floorboard, secret love letters that touchingly depict Ladell Allen's forbidden, heart-searing romance—and shed light on her tragic end.

978-0-7387-3073-8, 240 pp., 5³⁄₁₆ x 8　　　　　　　　　**$15.95**

To order, call 1-877-NEW-WRLD
Prices subject to change without notice
Order at Llewellyn.com 24 hours a day, 7 days a week!